Nations and Peoples

Japan

Japan

E. W. F. TOMLIN

with 29 illustrations and 2 maps

WALKER AND COMPANY
NEW YORK

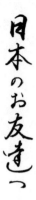

To my friends in Japan

© Thames and Hudson Ltd. 1973

Library of Congress Catalog Card Number: 72-87517

ISBN 0-8027-2127-3

First published in the United States of America in 1973
by the Walker Publishing Company, Inc.

Printed and bound in Great Britain

Author's note

I should like to thank Dr Carmen Blacker for kindly reading through the typescript and for making several valuable suggestions. Needless to say, any defects the book may contain are entirely my own responsibility.

I wish also to thank my sister, Miss E. M. Tomlin, for great help with the index, and my son, W. S. Tomlin, for valuable assistance with the Who's Who.

In the text, Japanese words are given a macron (e.g. Jōdo) where appropriate, except in the case of well-known place names, and words that enjoy an international usage (e.g. Judo). In the index and glossary, words preceded by the honorific o- are listed under their first letter.

Contents

1   Prehistory and myth

OF THE GREAT MOVEMENTS associated with European history – renaissance, reformation, revolution – the countries of the Orient have experienced no equivalent; or they have undergone such movements so recently as to leave intact a certain spiritual or cultural core. In the Indian sub-continent and in certain countries of South-East Asia, the conquest by a Western power did not destroy the national identity. Nor has the capture by a Western ideology of mainland China caused the moral and spiritual convulsion that might have been expected. The ideal ruler envisaged by Confucius, interpreting the 'mandate of heaven', has found a new incarnation in the poet-revolutionary Mao Tse-tung. As to Japan, she has enjoyed a *continuity* of history and culture almost without parallel. Admittedly, she has had her full share of alien influence. She has indeed gone out in search of it, as part of a planned policy. If the Greeks, or the Ionians, invented cultural relations in the West, Japan invented them in the East. At the beginning of her nationhood, Japan 'imported' Chinese culture, just as she deliberately imported Western culture and technology after the Meiji Restoration of 1868. If she has known how to absorb foreign influence, however, she has known also how to resist it. The one process involved the other, because both were deliberate. Consequently, when for the first time she was militarily subdued, at the end of the last war, she was still in a position to take or reject what she wished. This enabled her to survive a crisis that might otherwise have destroyed her.

We know comparatively little of the early history of Japan, for so far as the Japanese themselves are concerned, prehistory is a recent subject of study. J. H. Breasted rightly spoke of the New Past, referring to the wealth of knowledge gained by recent archaeological discovery, especially in Egypt and Sumeria. Japanese archaeology is concerned with the Newest Past; for until the surrender of 1945, the official past of Japan belonged not to history but to mythology. Furthermore, the mythology was particularly difficult for the Westerner to grasp. Highly complex and full of contradictions, it is quite unlike the mythology of any other people. Nevertheless, there are certain aspects of it which, properly interpreted, throw light upon the early development of the country; confirm the already impressive archaeological record; and go some way to explaining the psychology of the people.

Once firmly established in a culture, ' totem and taboo ' take a long time to lose their efficacy. In the West, there still exists a prejudice against eating horsemeat, because the early Christian evangelists wished to stamp out the pagan worship of the horse. How strong are certain sexual taboos may be judged from the fact that they survive despite the pressure of the most imperative of instincts, and of much relaxation of standards. The Japanese ideal of 'social harmony' *(wagō)* is due not to some happy disposition on the part of the people, but most probably to principles early inculcated by Shintō doctrine. The Finns, who are thought by some to be distantly related to the Japanese, display a contrary tendency, a yearning for solitude. Similarly, the notions of *on, giri*, and *oyabun-kobun* no doubt have their source in similar early indoctrination. *On* may be rendered as a state of ' indebtedness'; *giri* as ' duty' or ' obligation'; *oyabun-kobun* as the all-embracing and hierarchical system of personal relationships which make up Japanese (male) society. Hence the famous ' paternalism '. These are *social* imperatives; they play a part in Japanese life, and not least in Japanese politics, which, if less strong than in the past, must not be underestimated. If these relations function satisfactorily, the result is social harmony or *wagō*. The Western reader may assume that such ideas represent no more than vague aspirations towards a social ideal; but if he should consult books on Japanese business methods, such as Boye De Mente's *How Business is Done in Japan* (1960), Robert Ballon's symposium *Doing Business in Japan* (1967) or books on politics by Japanese themselves, such as Maruyama Masao's *Thought and Behaviour in Modern Japanese Politics* (1963), he will find these ideas to be the foundation of everyday economic and political transactions.

It is often maintained that the new generation of Japanese, or the post-war Japanese in general, have repudiated the past, and that the traditional social compulsions no longer operate. On the contrary, it is perhaps truer to say that, over the past decade, there has been a slight reversion to traditional ways. 'The attention to the present supposes a permanent obligation of readjusting, reshaping or re-tuning the new situation with the whole.... The success of adapta-tion can be equated to the fulfilment of this goal.'[1] At several moments of their history, the Japanese have been thought ready to throw off their traditions wholesale. Writing at the beginning of this century, Basil Hall Chamberlain, who knew Japan better than most foreigners, declared that 'Old Japan is dead, and the only decent thing to do with the corpse is to bury it'; but a few lines later he remarked that 'it is abundantly clear to those who have dived beneath the surface of the modern Japanese upheaval that more of the past has been retained than has been let go . . . the national character persists intact, manifesting no change in essentials'.[2] This is as much as to say that Japan has been discovering new ways of remaining herself.

Indeed, although the traditional religions of Japan, Shintō and Buddhism, have tended to lose their influence with the people, especially the young, the traditional *mœurs* remain very strong. This is due partly to the powerful 'hold' of such traditions, and partly to the fact that Japanese religion, especially Shintō, was for so long identified with the Japanese state. The charisma of the monarchy is still very powerful, as recent events have proved; and, even if the Emperor is not a god, he is still in effect the high priest of Shintō. No one has formally abolished that office, as the Caliphate of Islam was formally abolished in 1923 by Kemal Atatürk. Nohara Komakichi wrote in his *True Face of Japan* (1936): 'As all our thoughts and aspirations cluster about the figure of the Emperor, as rice keeps body and soul together, and our ancestors, as we think, are always around us, we Japanese cannot be anything but Shintoists.' Since those words were written, Japan has undergone the biggest political convulsion in her history; but the sentiments expressed are probably still not untrue so far as the Japanese 'collective unconscious' is concerned.[3]

One reason why the Japanese psyche is still profoundly imbued with traditional doctrine is that the religions of Japan are not mutually exclusive. That is to say, it is possible to be a Shintoist, a

[1] For notes, see p. 157

9

Buddhist, and a Taoist at one and the same time. One is married according to Shintō rites and buried according to Buddhist rites, though it is possible to be married according to Buddhist rites too, and some couples have recently requested a Christian wedding, though holding no specific Christian beliefs. Nevertheless, Shintō is essentially a religion for the group, making for *wagō*, while Buddhism is for the individual. Whereas a Japan without Buddhism is conceivable, a Japan without Shintō would be another country altogether. Hence the Japanese antipathy to the extremes of individuality. According to Shintō doctrine, individuality is that which invites the attention of the *kami*, or gods; and while this may be for good, it is usually for bad, so that the risk is rarely worth taking. When Dr Batchelor's adopted Ainu daughter became a Christian, her Japanese friends accused her, not of heresy or apostasy, but of *individualism*. She was 'on her own'; and that is still a dangerous path for a Japanese to tread.

What, then, is Shintō? The word derives from *shin*, god, and *tō*, way, so that the word signifies 'the way of the gods'. It was so called to distinguish it from another way, 'the way of the Buddha', Butsudō. In fact, there was no single name for this faith before the arrival of Buddhism.

Early Shintō belief, despite its emphasis upon purification and lustration, is said to have been little concerned with moral purity. According to more than one specialist,[4] between physical and moral rectitude, the distinction was made as late as the fourteenth century; but this is perhaps to project into early Shintō belief a distinction between mind and body which was not altogether clear. Some conception of good and bad is probably as old as mankind. It is doubtful whether the Egyptian *maat* (righteousness), which Breasted claimed to be the earliest moral concept, was conceived as *late* as he said it was in his *Dawn of Conscience* (1920). Consequently, the emphasis on purity in early Shintō was probably a quasi-moral concept. The devotee bathed or cleansed himself because this was symbolic of some sort of 'purity', which alone was pleasing to the gods. Possibly the so-called emergence of the moral-physical distinction marked the beginning of a form of secularism, just as the belief that the gods were in 'heaven' marked the end of an era when they were thought to inhabit, though in invisible form, the same world as mankind. It is a short step from separating heaven and earth to regarding heaven as a fiction, and earth as therefore deprived of all divinity. In that sense, the higher religions themselves may have been responsible for the rise of secularism, whereas a folk-religion such as Shintō preaches that much of nature is divine: stones, water, wood, organisms, and indeed men's artifacts may possess a *kami*, the original meaning of which was merely 'superior'. The *kami* descended into objects whose shape or constitution was pleasing to them. That most people have a residual Shintoism in their psychic make-up is very likely; for a mechanistic universe, while acceptable to the intellect, is abhorrent to the sensibility.

In modern Japan, though many thousands of Shintō shrines exist, a number are neglected for lack of means towards their upkeep, and the priests have to take on other jobs to help make ends meet. The outward aspect of a shrine is often sombre, because the wood of which it is built is coarse, unvarnished, and unpainted or unstained. From the religious point of view, there is no particular virtue in preserving an old shrine. As at the Grand Shrine at Ise, the custom is to rebuild it every so often, preserving the traditional design; for it is a sign of neglect and impurity to allow a patina to form.

The organization of shrines is largely independent, though this was not always so. There is no central administration, no hierarchy of priesthood, and no systematic theology. In the decades before the last war, a nationalist form of Shintō was cultivated, centring round Emperor-worship. Consequently, after the war was over, Shintō as a nationalistic belief, with its fanatical devotion to the Emperor, was largely discredited. Even so, a warm loyalty or *chū* is still encouraged, not least by the Ministry of Education.

It is therefore true to say that the Emperor's status was closely involved with the traditional mythology, even though his personal divinity was a later invention. This mythology can be analysed into two strands, a solar worship and a creation story. The highest Shintō deity was the Sun Goddess, Amaterasu Ōmikami. (When St Francis Xavier came to Japan in 1549, he reported that the Japanese worshipped the sun.) The myth, highly simplified, runs as follows. Amaterasu Omikami had a younger brother, Susa-no-o, who rebelled against her. He made havoc, among other things, of his sister's rice fields. Rice has always been a sacred food for the Japanese. In consequence, Amaterasu retired to a cave in heaven. The lesser Shintō gods then set about deciding how to entice her out. Dances were performed in front of the cave: then a hymn was sung. As a result, the Sun Goddess emerged, and the world became warm and bright again. (Later, two families or clans, the Nakatomi and the Imibe, meaning 'ministers of the middle' and 'guild of abstainers' respectively, claimed descent from these gods.) As a punishment for his sin of desecration, Susa-no-o was banished for ever from the company of the *kami*.

That was not the end of the story. On leaving heaven, Susa-no-o's destination was an interesting one. He went to the region of Izumo, a town on the Japan sea coast of Honshu, not far from Matsue. Here he became the ruler, and here the Earth God was worshipped. By contrast, the cult of the Sun Goddess was established at Ise, in the region then known as Yamato. According to tradition, Izumo finally submitted to the authority of Ise; but even today the Emperor, whose personal shrine is Ise, may not enter the inner precincts of the Izumo shrine.

It would therefore seem that the mythology symbolizes or reflects a true historical rivalry, ending with the domination of the Yamato emperors. The imperial forces had apparently advanced to Yamato from Kyushu, the southernmost island, where the descent of the Sun Goddess to earth is still commemorated. The first emperor, supposedly descended from the Sun Goddess, was given the posthumous title of Jimmu, meaning 'divine warrior.' Jimmu is no doubt a mythical figure, just as the date of the beginning of his reign, 11th February 660 B C, is an arbitrary date; but the present Emperor of Japan is, so far as we can tell, descended from the early rulers of Yamato, thus making the Japanese monarchical system the oldest in the world.[5] The dynasty proper probably dates from the third century A D.

In early mythology, the Sun Goddess is represented as presiding over a flourishing economy, which was much like that of ancient Japan, though situated in a divine realm and inhabited by many other gods. The origin of Amaterasu Ōmikami herself belongs to the older creation story. This story concerns a brother and sister, Izanagi and Izanami, who, descending to earth, produced by their incestuous union the Japanese islands, together with some other gods. Izanagi had difficulty in giving birth to one god in particular, that of fire. The result was that she died. She descended to the lower world, where her brother visited her; but she was so ashamed to be seen in a condition of decay that she besought him to leave. As for Izanagi, he felt the need to purify himself. From the clothes which he discarded, and from other parts of his body, new gods were formed. These included the Sun Goddess, a Moon God, and Susa-no-o himself, who, as god of destruction, later behaved in the manner described. It is a curious and often muddled story, and it represents Japan as having been created before the Sun Goddess, who was to become the national protector. It is not uncommon for creation myths to be distinct from other primordial myths, but the two Japanese traditions have been deliberately blended.

Although the Earth God was worshipped at Izumo, and although in October *all* the Japanese gods are supposed to go to Izumo for an annual assembly (so that October is called 'the month without gods'), the Sun Goddess did not permit the descendants of Susa-no-o to rule the world. She decided that her grandson, Ninigi-no-Mikoto, should undertake this task, and she therefore sent down an embassy of gods to prepare the way for him. Some of these gods went to Izumo, where, in an interview with one of Susa-no-o's sons, Ōna-mochi, they demanded that the land should be surrendered to the Sun Goddess. Although at first he refused, a compromise was at length arrived at whereby Ōnamochi should look after spiritual affairs and Ninigi-no-Mikoto should deal with civil government. Ninigi-no-Mikoto then landed in Kyushu, bringing with him a curved jewel, an iron sword and a bronze mirror. These were a token of the right of the Sun Goddess to rule Japan from heaven and her descendants to rule Japan on earth. To this day, the Emperor's regalia consists of a jewel, a sword, and a mirror.

Such was the 'official teaching' – and the source of much chauvin-istic propaganda – until very lately. That is the reason why it is not preposterous to dwell upon the influence of this mythology on the Japanese character. Light, purity, cleanliness are values in Japan, whereas there is a taboo against death as well as decay, at least in Shintō doctrine.

To what extent such a mythology was 'believed in' by the ordinary man is difficult to say. Even the most rationalist-minded Japanese, when visiting a shrine, will clap his hands dutifully to attract the attention of the god or gods, and remain to pray for a few moments. The habits of generations cannot be renounced as a result of a formal edict of 'disestablishment', such as the Americans pronounced against Shintō at the beginning of the Occupation; and it is likely that this cluster of beliefs, so beautiful in many respects, will be nurtured for centuries to come, if only as the basis of ritual which the ordinary person cannot bring himself to discard.

Let us now turn from myth to history. Clearly the parable of the rivalry between Ise and Izumo is concerned with events which, viewed from another angle, are comparatively recent. Before the Japanese peoples came on the scene, who were the inhabitants of Japan? (The word Japan comes from the Chinese Jih-pen. The Japanese word is Nihon or Nippon, meaning 'the source of the sun'.) This is a subject of much controversy. A dwindling race called the Ainu still lives in the northern island of Hokkaido. Now it is generally agreed that the Ainu were the original inhabitants of the archipelago. Unlike the Japanese, they are a Caucasian or Caucasoid people, very hirsute, with whitish skin and brown eyes. Moreover, the Ainu language, now virtually extinct, is related to no other language, and this might suggest that it is one of the oldest of human tongues. Some scholars suggest that these people reached Japan 40 or 50 thousand years ago, via Siberia and Sakhalin (where some Ainu still remain); but this can be no more than conjecture.

On the other hand, we are beginning to find out more about those early human migrations which, instead of being haphazard, were to some extent *planned*. This was due to a number of factors, not least the control of the food supply whereby man became a food-producer instead of being a food-gatherer. There are traces of such migrations, perhaps partly impelled by population-pressure, as having moved from the Caspian basin across Afghanistan through the Khyber Pass and into the valley of the Indus; or moving across Turkestan to the upper Yellow River valley into the heart of China and thence to Korea and Japan; or passing across Siberia along the Amur river and via Sakhalin down into Hokkaido. The people who were on the move would not have practised the techniques of the people they left behind; for the centres from which the movements spread, and at which some of them halted, formed probably the most stable societies. Nor must we assume absolute ethnic homogeneity; there would be stragglers and much intermixture. Nevertheless, an ethnic core, so to speak, would be preserved in the form of a tribal system of increasing rigidity. The tribes would primarily consist of hunters and fishers in the old nomadic tradition.

The possibility that the Ainu, or rather their ancestors, occupied at one time the whole of Japan is reinforced not merely by the existence of Ainu place-names but by a number of recent archaeological discoveries. These discoveries have to do with a Neolithic culture to which the name Jōmon has been associated. Jōmon means 'corded pattern', and it is used because such patterns have been found on pottery of remarkable beauty, though the people who made them had apparently no knowledge of the potter's wheel.

Sites identified as Jōmon, and yielding recognizable and distinctive artefacts in addition to pottery, have been found in Kyushu, the southernmost island; in increasing numbers in Honshu; and, most pervasive of all, in Hokkaido. The earliest of these sites date probably from the beginning of the Neolithic Age, which was about 10,000 B C.[6] Some of them seem to have been occupied until about 200 B C in the Kansai region (i.e., that of Kyoto and Nara), but a good deal later farther north. Meanwhile, according to the evidence, another culture, clearly distinguished from the Jōmon by its use of bronze and iron, and also by its cultivation of rice, had begun to flourish. It did so chiefly in Kyushu from about the first century B C; but hardly at all, judging from the scarcity of traces, in Hokkaido. This is known as the Yayoi culture, named after the place where the first remains were found, that is to say, one of the campuses of the University of Tokyo. The Yayoi culture lasted until about the fourth century A D. (Yayoi pottery has also been found in Southern Korea, whence these people may possibly have come.) Now, as we have seen, the Japanese state was beginning to consolidate itself in the Yamato region at about this time: which may explain both the rapid disappearance or assimilation of the Yayoi people and the gradual retreat of the Jōmon people northward. Of this northerly movement we have abundant evidence. It is interesting that the latest Jōmon pottery (there are five main periods), namely spouted vessels, has been found predominantly in the north-east.

In the Japanese records known as the *Kojiki* and the *Nihon Shoki*, compiled in the eighth century, there are references to people called the Ebisu, or Emishi, who were in occupation of the north of Honshu; and although these records contain much myth, we have evidence that the Japanese were constantly at war with the Ainu at least from 733 onwards, when Akita was a garrison town.[7] In another chronicle, the *Fudoki*, there is mention of vast shell-heaps, which the annalist attributes to the presence of a race of giants. In another passage, concerning the year 839, the annalist refers to piles of stone arrowheads, which he regarded as of similar origin. Such accumulations of shells and arrow-heads (the latter of obsidian), harpoon heads and fish-hooks are now familiar features of Jōmon sites. At the Kasori site, some way out of Tokyo, an enormous quantity of shells has been brought to light, in the proximity of dwellings which in design resemble the traditional Ainu house.

The identification of the Jōmon and the ancient Ainu has been challenged by a number of experts, both Japanese and foreign; but there are some reasons for assuming that the two peoples were the same, especially as the Jōmon are thought to be a branch of an early people who wandered over the coniferous forest zone of North Asia. Between traditional abstract designs on Ainu handicrafts and Jōmon designs on pottery and burial figurines there is a remarkable resemblance. Secondly, the Jōmon, unlike other developed Neolithic peoples, seem to have possessed little, if any, systematic knowledge of agriculture and animal husbandry. They were a people who subsisted on the food nearest to hand, namely shells and nuts. Other evidence, such as the brief periods during which many Jōmon sites were inhabited, suggests a people who were constantly on the move. No doubt the pressures under which the Jōmon or their successors lived, while the Japanese people gained power and unity, made their acquisition or retention of basic techniques difficult or impossible: for agriculture and animal husbandry require prolonged and relatively undisturbed settlement. Living under similar pressure for most of their history, the Ainu remained hunters and fishers – dwelling in hunting villages and fishing villages – until such time as, under Japanese instruction, they acquired agricultural techniques. In fact, the Ainu were forbidden to hunt and fish from 1884 onwards, with consequent disruption of their cultural traditions.

These traditions were associated with a religion of great interest. The Ainu worshipped a number of gods or *kamui*: we do not know whether this word was borrowed from the Japanese or whether the Japanese borrowed it from the Ainu. Among these deities, *kamui-fuchi* was accorded special veneration. This *kamui-fuchi* was a female deity, the 'Supreme Ancestress', as Neil Gordon Munro, the Ainu expert, called her. Possibly this deity was that same Mother Goddess who would seem to have been worshipped by the Jōmon; for the figurines found in Jōmon tombs were unquestionably female, some being represented as pregnant. (Such figurines have been unearthed only in northern Honshu and Hokkaido.) Possibly again this Mother Goddess was akin to that worshipped by the inhabitants of certain pre-Hittite peoples of Anatolia; for there is reason to believe that the Mother Goddess was one of the archetypal deities of humanity in the epoch prior to the rise of the higher religions. Nor is her worship extinct today, even in the most exclusive of them. Now there are signs that Jōmon society was a matriarchy, as was the traditional Ainu society.

There is also a remarkable similarity between the ancient Ainu dwellings – particularly in respect of the central hearth sunk in the ground, the fixed position of the sacred emblems in the north-east corner, and the sacred window in the east through which nothing might be thrown and no one should look – and that of the Jōmon huts or pit-dwellings. Both dwellings formed temple-habitations. There were no Ainu shrines and no Ainu priesthood, though there is some evidence of Shamanism. Munro's account of the religious importance of the Ainu hearth, with its sacred embers, indicates its function as the focus of religious practice and ritual: which, if these went back (as seems probable) to the Neolithic period, would lend further weight to the view that the Jōmon were forerunners of the Ainu. Moreover, the word *Fuji* is an Ainu word meaning 'fire'; for *Kamui-fuchi* was also Goddess of Fire and of the hearth, enjoying the special role of mediatrix with the other *kamui*. Indeed, the Ainu house was peculiarly her temple. Ainu women used to tattoo their mouths, the incisions being filled with soot, which was regarded as a sacred substance, protective of the mouth and nose from evil spirits. The figurines found in Jōmon tombs show evidence of markings which bear a resemblance to such tattooing.

Despite these remarkable parallels, there is at present insufficient proof that the Jōmon were the ancient Ainu, though authorities such as Sir George Sansom have pointed out that the 'study of human remains found in Neolithic sites in Japan . . . shows that they were of the same physical type as the modern Ainu'. Indeed, if the Jōmon and the Ainu are two wholly distinct people, the question arises where the Ainu came from and when. Apart from the Mongols, there is no evidence of foreign invasion of the archipelago in historical times; and the fact that Ainu names are found all over

Japan – the old word for 'Kyushu' was *Tsukushi*, which may derive from the Ainu *chiu-kushii*, meaning 'a rapid stream or crossing-place'[8] – proves that these people have been in Japan for several thousands of years.

One reason why some Japanese experts are reluctant to identify the Jōmon with the ancient Ainu is that, so far as it has been unearthed, the Jōmon culture seems to have been highly developed, at least in an aesthetic sense; and from the time when they began fighting the Ainu, the Japanese have tended to regard the former as a people both primitive and even decadent. It is true that for several centuries, and at least since the Matsumae clan were put in charge of Hokkaido, the Ainu have been showing signs of demoralization. In the seventeenth century, there was an outburst of 'Arctic hysteria',[9] in which hundreds of Ainu, stripped naked, 'danced' their way into the mountains and there perished; and travellers in Hokkaido in the nineteenth century, such as Isabella Bird (Mrs Bishop), Savage Landor, and John Batchelor, reported that the Ainu were much given to *sake*-drinking. Without doubt, the break-up of their way of life in the 1880's, due to the ban on hunting and fishing, was a further blow to their morale. On the other hand, observers such as Munro, who studied Ainu culture while it was still in some degree 'living', argued that it was of unique value and interest; and there may be a case for believing that its uniqueness stems from the fact that it is one of the *oldest* cultures extant. Owing to enlightened Japanese policy of recent years, and to much research and salvage work by specialists, the remaining Ainu, who number no more than a few hundreds, have regained their self-respect; and the Ainu men and women whom one may meet in Hokkaido are a handsome, proud and gentle people. Yet they have no future as a distinct race. So far as language and education are concerned, they are virtually integrated with the Japanese community; and Ainu girls feel that it is a step up in the world to marry a Japanese. Short of a deliberate policy of separate development, which would be objectionable from other points of view, it is difficult to see what can prevent the disappearance of the Ainu as an ethnic group within the next generation or two.

Intermediate between the northward movement of the Jōmon and the disappearance of the Yayoi was a culture, dating from about 300 A D, associated with enormous tombs or tumuli, where chiefs or kings lie buried. These tombs, some bigger than the great pyramid, were keyhole-shaped, containing a chamber lined with stone, in which a number of objects, including figurines or *haniwa*, have been found. More elaborate than those preserved in the Jōmon tombs, these figurines represent warriors in distinctive clothing, often on horseback, and the tombs of the later period contain a great deal of armour and horse-trappings, some made of gold. The construction of the tombs and the quality of their contents suggest a people of considerable skill and great powers of organization. They may have been basically Yayoi, and there is evidence that they were in touch with the mainland, especially with the kingdoms into which Korea was then divided. This culture is still, so to speak, being dug up.

Apart from the fact that Japanese archaeology is still a young science, the vagueness of our knowledge of this and the former period of Japanese history is due largely to the total absence of indigenous records. The late Jōmon, the Yayoi people, and the early Japanese had no system of writing, though it is difficult to know how government was carried on in its absence. The Sumerians and Egyptians possessed a sophisticated writing system several thousand years B C; but there is no trace of even so much as a notation or picture-language in Japan until the arrival of Chinese monks. For there were written records in both China and Korea; and it is from these that we are able to learn much about the early Japanese people and their system of government. In a chronicle dating from *c.* A D 297, entitled *A History of the Kingdom of Wei*, we gather that the land, called Wa, was divided into 100 communities. A later chronicle entitled *A History of the Latter Han Dynasty*, dating *c.* A D 445, speaks of a delegation from Wa to the Chinese court as early as AD 57. From the same chronicle it also seems apparent that a powerful ruler had taken control of a province called Yamatai; and there is still much debate as to whether Yamatai and Yamato are the same place. This ruler was female, and her name was either Pimiko or Himiko. Whatever the issue of such debatable problems, it is obvious that communications between Japan and Korea were close, and it is probable that the ruler of Japan dominated at least part of Korea. That might suggest that some writing was imported, if only to keep records, now lost. It is also obvious that of the numerous communities or clans into which Japan was at that time divided, the Yamato clan was emerging as the most powerful.

An expert on the history of Asia, Professor Egami Namio, holds that the Yamato emperor was not in fact a local ruler at all but a conqueror from abroad, namely, a horse-riding warrior of one of the Tungus tribes which, after the collapse of the Han Empire, invaded the Korean peninsula and established the 'Three Kingdoms'. He then crossed the Tsushima Straits, landed at Kyushu, and, subduing the people of Wa, set up his headquarters in Yamato. This would account for the objects, including horse-trappings, found in the late tumuli. It is also consistent with the mythical account of the conquering passage to Yamato of the emperor Jimmu.

The clans or *uji* were organized on two levels: there was an aristocracy, and below that, forming a complex but powerful infrastructure, a series of groups concerned with agriculture, fishing and craftwork. Moreover, each clan leader had a title. There were some clans which themselves specialized in an occupation, usually of a superior kind, which they undertook in the service of the Court. Each clan likewise had its own god, but above all these gods was the Sun Goddess herself. The emperor, as head of the Yamato clan, combined the offices of priest and ruler.

It is therefore apparent that Japanese society, when we first learn of it, was already highly organized. Despite the onset of 'times of troubles', this form of society held together, at least at its core, for many centuries, until the conduct and even the wearing-apparel of each class was subject to strict regulation. In this respect, there have been few societies to compare with it. And despite the greatly relaxed discipline, modern Japanese society still bears the marks of such 'training'. The survival of Japan as a cohesive community may well be attributable to it.

2 The Nara and Heian periods

BUDDHISM, which was introduced into Japan in the sixth century, probably about 552 but possibly in 534, met at first with bitter opposition; but gradually, and as a result of the missionizing of a remarkable personality, Prince Umayado (574–622), or Shōtoku Taishi, to use his posthumous name, it gained ground. Finally it came to terms with the traditional faith. Today, many Buddhist temples display Shintō features, and vice-versa; and, as for the Shintō gods, they came to be regarded as avatars of the Buddhist pantheon. This confluence of the two traditions was the more remarkable in that Buddhism, when it arrived in Japan, was already more than a thousand years old. Apart from its direct religious influence, Buddhism was a great bearer of culture; and behind the Chinese culture which it introduced was that of India, the country of the Buddha's birth.

The form of Buddhism to enjoy greatest prestige in Japan was the Mahayana, or 'Great Vehicle'. According to the Mahayana, the Buddha was himself a transcendent deity. As to Buddha, the man, he paid little attention to 'metaphysical' theology; his concern was to preach a doctrine whereby desire and suffering should be eliminated, and the way opened to Nirvana or the state of bliss. The idea that life was a half-real, half-dream experience has certainly exerted a profound influence on the Japanese mind, just as meditation and contemplation are practices to which the Japanese have become habituated. The earliest great Buddhist temples were those built at Nara, the first planned capital (710); the Tōdaiji temple, with its great statue of the Buddha, or Daibutsu, is today among the oldest religious monuments in Japan. The Daibutsu was built first, and the temple buildings round it. The whole was also called the Great Kegon temple, after the sect which worshipped the universal Buddha (called, in Japanese, Roshana). Even so, the Sun Goddess's 'permission' had to be sought for the Daibutsu to be erected, and a holy monk, Gyōgi, head of the Hossō sect, made a special pilgrimage to Ise to ascertain her views. The Tōdaiji and other magnificent structures were built under the supervision of priests holding doctrines which must have been difficult for all but specialists to grasp, so that the laity derived their religious experience through imagery and ceremony. So great was the prestige of Buddhism during the Nara period (710-794), when there were six sects, that it served to uphold the power of the Emperor himself. This applied particularly to the Ritsu sect, which preached discipline and order, and through which Buddhism became virtually a national Church. Many Buddhist priests sought places at Court. At the same time, a network of temples and nunneries was organized in the provinces, some being integrated into the system of local government. In the early days, priestesses presided over certain Shintō shrines, especially that of Ise, but later the status of many of these priestesses declined. Buddhist nunneries, on the other hand, have always enjoyed high prestige, and many exist today, such as the beautiful Hokkeji nunnery at Nara, which is under imperial patronage.

In due course, Nara Buddhism, despite the great artistic flowering which it stimulated (the *Shōsōin* near the Tōdaiji is still a store of artistic treasures, mostly those used at its dedication in 752), came to assume a somewhat worldly character; and this was one of the reasons – another was the power acquired by a line of empresses – why the capital, after an interval of ten years at Nagaoka, today a somewhat featureless town, was transferred to Heian-Kyō, later called Kyoto. This ushered in the famous Heian period (794-1185). During this period, Buddhism underwent a renaissance, due chiefly to the rise of two 'mountain sects': the Tendai sect with its headquarters on Mount Hiei overlooking Kyoto, and the Shingon sect with its headquarters on Mount Kōya in the Kii province. The Tendai sect attached particular importance to the Lotus Sutra, which it claimed to be the quintessence of Buddhist teaching, whereas the Shingon sect preached a doctrine of such extreme complexity that, once again, the faithful needed a superb art on which to nourish their religious sensibility. Today, Mount Kōya is still a treasure-house of religious art, and thousands of visitors patronize the temples, even though the degree of genuine Buddhist devotion may have declined.

During the Middle Heian Period, which lasted from about 967 to 1068, a new cultural crystallization occurred, though this was confined to the aristocrats at the Court at Heian-Kyō. Perhaps at no time has life been lived so consistently at the level of aesthetic refinement.[1] As to the lower classes, their lot was naturally a hard one; for it was they who toiled to sustain the aristocracy's high standard of living. Much literature, including one of the world's great novels, *The Tale of Genji*, was produced by Court ladies. In contrast to male authors, Lady Murasaki (Murasaki Shikibu) and Sei Shōnagon, author of *The Pillow Book*, wrote not in the Chinese character but in the Japanese syllabary known as *hiragana*. This meant the use of Japanese instead of Chinese for literature: hitherto Chinese had been employed for all serious work. Both Lady Murasaki and Sei Shōnagon expressed attitudes to life which have themselves greatly influenced the Japanese character. To define *aware*, the mood expressed by Lady Murasaki, is difficult on account of its subsequent shift of meaning. In *The Tale of Genji*, it implies an exquisite sensibility, a delicate culture of the feelings, but with an underlying sense of the ephemeral nature of experience,[2] whereas today it would be rendered as 'grief'. Sei Shōnagon, by contrast, displays *okashi*, or what we might call 'a pretty wit'. The Japanese still regard sensibility and lightness of touch as superior to rationality and down-to-earth judgment. The quality of their life is thereby subtly different in kind from that of the Westerner.

In the so-called Kamakura Period (1185-1333), when the Kyoto aristocracy had lost much of its authority, new and more popular forms of Buddhism arose. These were developments chiefly of Tendai theology. Jōdo or Pure Land Buddhism was a doctrine accessible to all: the faithful needed merely to call upon the name of Amida Buddha, by an invocation termed *nembutsu*, in order to obtain spiritual succour. Moreover, if fervent in this practice, they would earn a place after death in the Western paradise or Pure Land, where they would spend eternity seated on lotus blossoms in a pool in front of Amida's throne. Such a doctrine would seem to be simple enough; but the simplicity was taken a stage further in a particular sect of Jōdo, called Jōdo Shinshū or true Pure Land doctrine. Jōdo Shinshū proved highly popular among the peasants, the class immediately below that of the warriors. In contrast to the appealing doctrine of Jōdo was Nichiren Buddhism, named after its founder.

Nichiren (1222-82), a militant preacher of a kind of chauvinist Buddhist doctrine, shared the Shingon devotion to the Lotus Sutra. His turbulent life and extravagant teaching not merely exerted great influence in his day, but survived to inspire a post-war nationalist and belligerent form of Buddhism called Sōka-Gakkai. Finally, the Kamakura Period and the later Ashikaga and Muromachi Periods saw the rise of another Buddhist doctrine which has exerted great influence, not least in the West. This was Zen.

Established in Japan by the Indian monk Daruma, Zen (a word derived from the Chinese *Cha'an*) is a blend of the Mahayana and Taoism. It is by no means an easy doctrine to define. Stress is placed on intuition and on the arrival at a state of instant illumination called *satori*. Such a state may be brought about by experiences of widely different kinds, among them being the propounding of paradoxes or *kōans*; but the chief aid to the attainment of *satori* is intensive, though not necessarily intense, meditation undertaken in a sitting posture *(zazen)*. The propounding of *kōans* was stressed above all by the Rinzai sect, of which the founder was Eisai (1141-1215); *zazen* was the chief practice of the Sōtō sect, founded by Dōgen (1200-53). Without doubt, the Sōtō has enjoyed the greater popularity; today many Japanese, including the young, undergo annual courses of meditation, even if they are not strictly 'believers', because the technique of meditation is congenial to them.

Some Westerners have endeavoured to practise Zen in the hope of achieving a short-cut to *satori*; but it would seem that the real attraction is towards a method which promises to relieve the devotee of the necessity of using his intellectual faculties – hence the association of Zen, at least in the West, with other supposed short-cuts to insight, such as drug-taking. So far as the Westerner is concerned, the practice of *zazen*, like that of Yoga, is finally of little value without some knowledge of the doctrinal background of these techniques (Yoga, for instance, is one of several doctrines of Vedanta). Arthur Koestler has well described the situation:

> The great Zen masters were, after all, sages with a shrewd knowledge of character; they knew that the cosmic nihilism of their doctrine was like arsenic – in small doses a stimulant, in large doses poison. Their wisdom found an unexpected confirmation several centuries later, when Zen was exported and let loose

among intellectuals. . . . They tried hard to obey its command: 'Let your mind go and become like a ball in a mountain stream': the result was a punctured tennis-ball surrounded by garbage, bouncing down the current from a burst water-main.[3]

Zen gave rise to a new school of art and culture in general. The origin of the Noh drama is obscure. Like the mystery or miracle plays of the West, it probably began as a form of religious ritual. Zeami, the first great writer of Noh plays, lived from 1363 to 1443 (or 1445), and the Noh drama thenceforth became as popular with the warriors as Zen. Today, there is a revival of interest in the Noh, similar perhaps to the renewed popularity before and after the war of poetic religious drama in the West. Noh societies have sprung up in the big towns, and performances at great shrines such as Miyajima, near Hiroshima, are attended not merely by intellectuals but by the common people, who follow the archaic language in specially-edited texts. About the time of the rise of the Noh, *Cha-no-yu* or Tea Ceremony was developed. This originated in association with the practice of Zen meditation, being a necessary and welcome refreshment after the effort of concentration. Today, the religious aspect of the Tea Ceremony has tended to give place to the aesthetic; but ceremonies, usually much shorter than the traditional ones (which might last as long as four hours), are still held in temples and elsewhere. Otherwise, skill in the ceremony, with its carefully prescribed movements and with its treasured utensils, is regarded as an essential part of the education of girls, a certificate of proficiency being a useful qualification for marriage. The same holds good of the popular art of ikebana, or flower arrangement. Training in these arts, like training by young men in martial arts such as judo or aikidō, may occupy years. To the serious practitioner, they form part of a way of life, even though the overtly religious aspect may have receded into the background.

3   The rise of the military class

ALTHOUGH SUCH ARTS, observances and elegant pastimes played an important part in social life – perhaps a bigger part than in any other civilization – the Japanese people, from the Heian period onwards, was very far from being a stable, still less a contented, society. The refined life at Court had imposed a heavy burden on the countryside; but, as there was gradual central stagnation, so there was by contrast provincial activity and development. The country was divided into a patchwork of estates. From the yield in kind of these estates the workers, managers and owners drew their livelihood. In fact the real authority still rested with certain branches of the Imperial family and nobility, though as these were now virtually cut off from the Court, they assumed names of their own, while not averse to boasting their royal connection. Hence arose the Minamoto and the Taira families, which also bore the name of Genji and Heike. These families, like the other provincial aristocrats, wielded above all military authority. Their leaders were mounted knights, equipped with bows and arrows, and they collectively played a part similar to that of the early clans or *uji*. Moreover, each knight had his retainer or retainers; and these 'servants', or samurai, were bound to their masters in a special way. The samurai finally formed an aristocracy of their own.

Between the Minamoto and the Taira families there came to be increasing rivalry. The chief ambition of each family was to gain influence at Court, where another family, the Fujiwara, had been long the power behind the throne. It was finally a member of the Taira family, Kiyomori, who triumphed after two brief but bloody wars. According to custom, he married his daughters into the Imperial line, and, as an added precaution, into the Fujiwara family as well. As the realization of his ambition, he lived to see his own grandson ascend the throne.

Unfortunately for Kiyomori, the Minamoto family was still powerful in the provinces. Nor did they lack allies among some of the Taira themselves. After Kiyomori's death in 1181, a host led by Yoritomo threatened Kyoto, and the Taira were obliged to take the emperor, still a child, to safety in the island of Shikoku. After a brief internecine conflict between the Minamoto themselves, a young man, Yoshitsune, who had been brought up in a monastery, took command of the advance against the Taira. He had a series of spectacular successes. Catching the Minamoto in a cavalry attack near modern Kobe, he crossed the Inland Sea, and routed them at their Shikoku base. In this encounter, the young Emperor was drowned. Moreover, the sword, which with the mirror and the jewel formed the imperial regalia, was lost. (Fortunately, it was a duplicate.) Yoshitsune later became a semi-legendary figure and was worshipped as an Ainu god.

The triumph of the Minamoto under Yoritomo resulted in the acknowledgment of one authority over much of central and western Japan. Many of the estates, especially those owned by the Taira, went to his followers. A feudal system came into being in which the estates were supervised by stewards who, though not the legal owners, came to form a hereditary class. It was they who effectively administered the provinces and provided for their defence. Above them were so-called 'protectors', who constituted civil governors; they also became hereditary. This tightly-knit but not always regular system was controlled from a new base; for, wishing to keep himself and his followers apart from the aristocracy at Kyoto, Yoritomo set up his government at Kamakura, not far from Edo (Tokyo). Such was the residual prestige of the Kyoto government, however, that Yoritomo still deferred to it on major matters. After all, his government was at first a family affair, given the extended meaning of 'family' at that time; but in due course the Kyoto government gave him a title which had for several centuries been conferred upon generals specially delegated to keep at bay the Ainu 'barbarians'. This was Shogun, or Generalissimo, or, to give it its full name, 'barbarian-quelling Generalissimo'. Thereby Yoritomo and his Kamakura government acquired, in all eyes, a measure of legality. This ingenious system, with the Emperor reigning in the background and the Shogun assuming overt rule, was thereafter to become the pattern of Japanese administration, though there were occasions when members of the Imperial family acted as Shoguns. To it may be ascribed the survival of the Emperor system. Even so, the Shogun's government, powerful though it might be, and hereditary as it became, was never thought of in law save as provisional. Hence the title *Bakufu* (literally 'tent government') for its administrative machine, whereas the civil government was still, by a fiction, associated with that of Kyoto.

Although the Kamakura Shogunate exerted firm, even severe, military rule, it was a period, as we have seen, of remarkable cultural flowering. The warrior's tastes, as so often in Japan, were often refined, tending sometimes towards the mystical. This alliance between the military caste and the bearers of culture – this association of military life with the arts, and the development of martial arts designed to promote spiritual development – was characteristic of Japan for many centuries. Its influence is still felt in the national life, with its peculiar combination of gentleness and strength, its underlying tendencies towards violence matched by the cultivation of elegance and delicacy.

Japanese history, from now on, is nothing if not complicated. Although the Shogunate was a Minamoto creation, the Minamoto family died out prematurely, largely owing to family quarrels and assassinations; and another family, the Hōjō, who were in fact descended from the Taira, took control. Since the Minamoto had depended initially on family loyalty, the survival of the Shogunate, though in other hands, testified to the effectiveness of the system it had created. At one point, however, even the Shogun's power was exercised by a regent, until, in order to regularize the situation, a child of the Fujiwara family from Kyoto was brought to Kamakura in 1219 to act as Shogun, at least in name. Later, the Hōjō, ambitious yet anxious to preserve legitimacy, brought from Kyoto members of the Imperial family to act, as indicated, as Shoguns. There were four of them. This did not prevent a curious turn of events in 1221 when there was a rebellion led by the Emperor Go-Toba[1] against Kamakura. This was known as the Shōkyū war. The rebellion was put down with vigour, and the Emperor's brother ascended the throne, though in the status of 'retired' – another curious fiction since he had never formally reigned. Determined to keep a closer eye over the Court, the Hōjō established two deputies there. Thus the power of the Shogunate increased, and the imperial line remained unbroken.

With communications difficult and the country in places only partly subdued, there was bound to be discontent and the recurring threat of revolt, even though the *Bakufu* and the Kyoto Court had achieved between them a kind of balance of power. In the year 1266, however, a challenge appeared not merely to the Hōjō but to Japan itself; and this challenge grew more serious in the years to follow. It came from the Mongol conqueror Kubilai, the Great Khan. In 1230, the Mongols had established themselves in China, breaking up the Sung Empire which had for more than 150 years maintained a civilization of a high order. Japan had kept in close touch with southern China, where the Sung still held sway, and they had relations even closer with Korea, though in neither case were the relations official – indeed, Korea was constantly harassed by Japanese pirates. At first, Kubilai dispatched a mission via Korea demanding that Japan should agree to pay tribute to him, and threatening invasion if she refused. Setting out in 1266, this mission failed to reach Japan, so another one was sent two years later.

Letters, addressed to the 'King of Japan', were handed to the representative of the *Bakufu* at Dazaifu in Kyushu. They were at once forwarded to Kamakura, whence they were forwarded as a matter of courtesy to the Court at Kyoto. Here the reaction was one of deep dismay. Apart from the threat which they contained, the letters displeased the Court by their insolent tone, being addressed to 'the king of a little country'. There were hasty consultations. Shrines were visited and the news 'reported' to the gods. A reply to the letters was then drafted, somewhat accommodating in tone, and dispatched for comment to Kamakura. Here a different mood prevailed. A young man of eighteen, Tokimune, had become regent. He was of firm and mature character. Aided by the sixty-year-old Masamura, who was a kind of assistant regent or 'co-signer', he decided that the Kyoto reply was too vacillating to send, especially as it contained little beyond the feeble statement that Japan, being a Land of the Gods, was ruled by a sacred dynasty not to be lightly treated. Instead of replying, the *Bakufu* ordered the envoys to return. This was not mere bravado. With measured confidence, the Shogunate began forthwith to prepare to defend Japan.

A third message, though there may possibly have been others, was sent by Kubilai in 1271. The Koreans, who again acted as mediators, took the opportunity of warning the Japanese of impending attack.

Admittedly, this was not done out of love for Japan; but the two peoples were now on better terms, since the Japanese had apologized for, and summarily dealt with, their pirates, and the Koreans, whose help Kubilai was trying to enlist, were not, as an occupied people, in a mood to welcome an extension of the Mongol power. Nevertheless, the Mongols, who were unfamiliar with sea transport and warfare, needed Korean help. They were given it, though with extreme reluctance.

The third message was dealt with in much the same way as the others. It was dispatched to Kyoto, answered there in draft, and reconsidered by the *Bakufu*. Meanwhile, all officials, the stewards and governors, in the Western region were ordered to man their posts, and the Western Defence Region in Kyushu was put on a war footing. Nearly a year later, in October 1272, a Mongol ambassador arrived. He made a peremptory request that he should be received in audience by the Emperor, but to this the *Bakufu* would not agree. He carried a letter which repeated the original demands, and insisted on an answer within two months. Again the letter was forwarded to the Court, and again the Court drafted a reply giving more than a hint of willingness to negotiate. The *Bakufu* would have none of this, and the ambassador was invited to take his leave. Clearly, this was a proof that Japan was prepared for hostilities.

All the evidence suggests that Kubilai had long prepared to take Japan by force. Yet when he finally set out in November 1274, eight years after the original demand for tribute, his invading army was not particularly large. It consisted of 15,000 Mongol and Chinese troops, preceded by a small advance guard. The latter was of high quality, but it was accompanied by a less well-equipped force of 8,000 Koreans. There were about 300 big ships, and a slightly larger number of small ones. These were manned by 7,000 Korean sailors, aided by a contingent of Chinese.

Two islands, Tsushima and Iki, were soon captured by the Mongols, after desperate resistance. The enemy then began to disembark at Hakata (19 November) and also at Imazu. The mobilization of the Western District was now complete, even though some vassals had failed to respond, and the Japanese launched an attack. Although they put up an impressive display of bravery, they were to some extent at a disadvantage, first, because they had among them no general with experience of full-scale warfare (the last big engagement had been the imperial rising against Kamakura in 1221), and secondly, because the knights were more accustomed to engaging in single combat, taking on adversaries of equal rank. As for the Mongols, they attacked, as was their habit, in close cavalry formation, with the assistance of catapults. These hurled missiles filled with combustible material, like small bombs. Nevertheless, the supply of arrows soon began to run short.

The Japanese managed to keep up their resistance throughout the day. Towards evening, they withdrew behind earthworks some miles inland. It was their one hope to hold the line until reinforcements should redress the temporary disparity in numbers. In fact, the situation underwent rapid and startling change during the night. A violent storm blew up. The Korean pilots, experienced in these waters, pointed out the danger of the ships being diverted or destroyed, and so the Mongol commander gave the order to re-embark. By morning, most of the invading force had managed to put to sea. How many ships were lost in the storm we do not know: Korean chroniclers say that at least 13,000 men died in the expedition as a whole, and of these the greater number may have been drowned. At all events, disaster of the first magnitude had overtaken the Mongol armada.

Whatever the reasons for the failure of the first Mongol invasion, Kubilai himself remained convinced that the disaster was due to nature and not to military incompetence. He therefore resolved to send yet another mission to Japan. On this occasion, his arrogance matched his self-confidence. He dispatched an envoy, this time proclaiming Japan a Mongol province and ordering the 'king of Japan' to come to his capital, the city later known as Peking. The message stung the *Bakufu* as much as it affronted the Kyoto Court. Instead of ordering the envoys to return, the *Bakufu*, on this and on a subsequent occasion, had them summarily executed. With the relations between the countries at their worst, it was necessary to prepare for another and no doubt more formidable attack. Work began on the construction of a great wall round Hakata Bay. Traces of this wall or earthwork, which took five years to build, can still be seen.

The Japanese were right to expect a force very different in strength and purpose from that which had arrived in 1274, even though intelligence had reached them that Kubilai had his hands full with other matters. Not merely was he endeavouring finally to occupy the Southern Sung domain, but he was having trouble in Korea, where there was a famine, due in part to the depredations of his own men. Indeed, we know that the Koreans did their best at one point to persuade Kubilai to change his mind about a second invasion of Japan. The *Bakufu*, realizing the difficulties of her enemies and their allies, even went so far as to consider profiting from the situation and mounting an offensive themselves, though in the end a compromise was reached, and a small naval force was made ready for the purpose merely of harassing the enemy. Meanwhile, patriotic fervour mounted. Prayers were said at shrines, offers of help poured in, the government introduced an austerity programme, and a body of experts, including members of the Hōjō family, came from Kamakura to inspect the Kyushu defences.

When the invasion took place, in 1281, it was on a huge scale. At least 140,000 men were involved, Mongol, Sung Chinese and Korean. The Koreans, having taken heart, had decided to contribute a fleet of their own. The invaders succeeded at first in occupying territory; but the wall held, and the Japanese took special precautions to see that it was not outflanked. In the bay, the Mongol junks, crowded together, were easy targets for the Japanese small craft. For seven weeks the fighting went on unabated. Then natural phenomena once more intervened. As suddenly as they usually do in August, a typhoon blew up. For two days its violence swept the coast of Kyushu until the Mongol fleet was in total confusion, and much of it wrecked. The beleaguered invaders on shore were put to frightful slaughter. This beneficent storm came to be known as the *kamikaze* or 'Divine Wind', an epithet revived in the last war, especially with reference to the Japanese suicide pilots. There are interesting parallels between the Mongol invasion, especially in its second phase, and that of the Spanish armada of 1588.

The over-all losses sustained on this expedition were enormous. The Chinese, whose heart can hardly have been in the war, suffered heavily. Although the Koreans had done their best to get their fleet away early, because they suspected what was coming, they are reported to have lost a third of their men, Koreans and Mongols. Of the 3,500 or so ships involved, the greater number foundered.

Notwithstanding this second reverse, Kubilai seems to have considered making a third expedition. He had established an 'Office for the Chastisement of Japan', and, as a world conqueror, he did not mean to be discouraged. Moreover, he had immense resources of manpower upon which to draw. Although the expedition he had organized was probably the largest ever assembled up to that time, he felt he could well surpass it. For their part, the Japanese did not relax their defences. During the next twenty years they remained vigilant. But Kubilai's military advisers managed finally to dissuade him from another attempt, though not until after he had made considerable preparations. Nor was Japanese soil occupied again until 1945.

The abortive Mongol invasions never ceased to stir the imagination of the Japanese. Some time about 1293, a pictorial account of the war was made on what came to be called the Mongol Scroll. This is so remarkable in its realism as to suggest that it was made, if not by some who had taken part in the fighting, then from accounts or sketches made by the participants. In it, individual warriors are recognizably portrayed, and their clothing and equipment are remarkably well depicted. The record is a fascinating one. In no other engagement on this scale were bows and arrows used in conjunction with 'bombs'.

The successful resistance to the Mongols confirmed the prestige of the warrior class. For while the Court had played its part in sustaining the morale of the people, it was the Kamakura Shogunate which had shouldered the major burden of defending the country. The code of fearlessness and of strict loyalty had proved itself in action. Personal loyalty was indeed a virtue which had been inculcated at every level. It formed the basis of the feudal system. The peasant served his lord with a devotion that exceeded loyalty to family. This, together with a certain innate stoicism, influenced the Japanese character to an extent that enabled such virtues to survive the collapse of feudalism, and indeed to endure into modern times.

An ideal of this kind will bring into being, by its very loftiness, a tendency in other directions. Thus Japanese history, especially the period under review, is marred by examples of betrayal and deception which might otherwise appear out of character. In the sphere of religion itself, the feudal virtues seemed to harmonize well with the Shintō doctrine; but in giving thanks for their deliverance from the Mongols, the Japanese honoured not merely the *kami*, in whose shrines they had made such fervent intercessions, but the Buddhist deities. The emperor Kameyama, in paying a special visit to the

33

Hachiman (war god) shrine of Iwashimizu, not far from Kyoto, caused to be read there extracts of the Buddhist scriptures.

Of the new developments in Buddhism which took place during this period, and of the importance for the warrior class of Zen and the Noh, we have spoken. It will not do to underestimate the influence which a discipline such as Zen exerted upon its more sincere devotees. Tokimune, the youth who took over the Regent's duties at the time of the threat of the first Mongol invasion, died at thirty-four. It is said that his marked composure of character was derived partly from a sedulous practice of Zen. His master was a Chinese monk who had come to Japan as a refugee from Mongol oppression in South China.

Tokimune was succeeded by his son, a boy of fourteen; but the Shogunate needed, after the war, a leader at least as stalwart as the father. Among those who in the enthusiasm of defending the country had spent large sums on equipping armies – for the vassals were obliged to raise forces at their own expense – there were stirrings of discontent. Many expected substantial rewards. Unfortunately, the *Bakufu* was in difficulties. Whereas in the case of family wars, such as that between the Minamoto and the Taira, the victor could draw upon a rich store of booty to compensate his loyal vassals, the *Bakufu* had no such pool of resources. The retainers were still obliged to undertake military service, but they were often hard put to it to afford the necessary equipment; and the situation was sometimes made worse by the fact that estates were divided not according to primogeniture but between the sons of landowners, who, with little to live on, still had to contribute their share of public service. A whole class of warrior-retainers thus sank into poverty and debt. Those few who managed to survive economically became focuses of loyalty for the less fortunate. Hence allegiance to Kamakura tended to decline, and a new group of leaders emerged. Owning large estates, this group came to play an important part in Japanese history. Its members assumed a position intermediate between the Shogunate at Kamakura and its nominal retainers. In due course, they became known as *daimyo*, feudal lords, though the word itself simply means 'great name'.

The warriors, who lived on fixed incomes based usually on rice, were not the only ones to complain of the *Bakufu*'s ingratitude. The religious foundations were also aggrieved. According to the opinion generally held, the Mongols had been defeated as a result of divine intervention; and this had been secured, so it was claimed, by the prayers offered up by shrines and temples. The Hōjō family, who were devout Shintoists and Buddhists, felt under a special obligation to the religious foundations; and what property could be drawn upon went to them rather .than to the warrior retainers. The latter put in applications for compensation which the *Bakufu* directed to lower authorities. The situation finally became intolerable. The *Bakufu* decided that it could consider no further applications for reward, and in 1294 it issued an edict to this effect. This was a heavy blow to the warrior class, and not least to those of Kyushu, who had been by far the most deserving. There was muttering, but no open revolt. Meanwhile, until the death of Kubilai, which occurred in 1294 and following which the danger of invasion receded, the retainers continued conscientiously to look to the defences of the country, especially in the south. Indeed, the Mongols, even without their great leader, remained fascinated by Japan, and in 1299, they sent a Zen monk over there as an emissary, possibly with a view to re-establishing good relations. In due course he became naturalized. Much good work of this kind was undertaken by Zen monks. Commercial relations were improved with South China, even though the economic situation of Japan was passing through a difficult phase.

In fact, what took place was the transfer of power from one class to another. As the prestige of the warrior class declined, so that of the merchant class rose. To it was transferred some of the property, with its attendant rights, which the warriors and retainers could no longer afford to maintain. Although this mercantile class was not yet a fully-fledged part of society, it was coming into being as a result of the social transformation. Those who had money lent it to those in need of it; and the warriors or retainers were precisely in such straits. Solicitous of their position, the *Bakufu* occasionally issued edicts fixing interest rates and cancelling debts. One special Act of Grace, dated 1297, forbade the transfer of estates or fiefs to those outside the *Bakufu*'s control and imposed restrictions on personal loans. This was a direct attack upon the merchant class, and the latter energetically responded by litigation. Within a short time the Act was rescinded, though others were promulgated later. The *Bakufu* was fighting an ineffective rearguard action which in the end led to its undoing.

The occasion, though not the cause, of the fall of the Kamakura Shogunate was an attempt by the Imperial Court to recover its power. This was similar, save in its partial success, to that made by the Emperor Go-Toba in 1221. The Emperor in question, named Go-Daigo, ascended the throne in 1318. He was one of two branches of the Imperial family claiming to be the rightful line, and in the resulting quarrel the Shogunate diplomatically suggested that the two houses should take turns in occupying the throne. As this was not to Go-Daigo's liking, he began to plot against Kamakura; and when the latter endeavoured to secure his abdication in favour of the other line, he started the revolt in 1331 which is known as the Genkō War. Go-Daigo was supported by the large monasteries and some local warriors. For although the Shogun's forces captured him and exiled him in 1332 to the Oki islands, off Matsue, the local lords, including a remarkable warrior, Kusunoki Masashige, who had deserted Kamakura in 1331 (though he strictly owed no allegiance thereto), continued resistance to the Shogun. In due course, other warriors joined in. In 1333, Go-Daigo escaped from exile. More surprises followed. The general sent by the Shogun to seize Go-Daigo suddenly changed sides and entered Kyoto as the Emperor's champion. This man, Ashikaga Takauji, was a descendant of the Minamoto. It was evidently his hope to become Shogun himself. Meanwhile, another descendant of the Minamoto, Nitta Yoshisada, attacked Kamakura. This spelt the end of the Hōjō power.

The Imperial house was to suffer too. Go-Daigo, feeling secure, proclaimed in 1334 a new era whereby his reign was to be called *Kemmu*, a time for the restoration of imperial rule. He appointed some of his generals as provincial governors. But the era was shortlived. In 1336, he was obliged to flee from Kyoto. His former ally, Ashikaga Takauji, had made another change of front, deciding to support his own candidate for the throne. He had quarrelled with his ally Nitta Yoshisada, who had continued to support the Emperor. Go-Daigo set up a separate capital at mountainous Yoshino, south of Nara. There he died in 1339, to be succeeded by Prince Norinaga, later called Go-Murakami. There were thus two Emperors and two capitals, and shortly after there was another Shogun; for Ashikaga Takauji, not without a struggle, had achieved his ambition in 1338.

The Ashikaga Shogunate, as it was called, lasted until 1573. It was still a feudal era, but the system differed in many respects from that

36

initiated by Yoritomo. There was no comparable loyalty between the Shogun and his personal retainers. The warriors had achieved a measure of independence. For the Shogun, it was a case of winning their support, and of ensuring that none among them should acquire excessive power. Moreover, the Ashikaga Shogunate set up no independent seat, as Yoritomo had done at Kamakura; its base was Kyoto. This led inevitably to greater contact and involvement with the Imperial Court. Like the Kamakura Shogunate, however, the Ashikagas had their deputies and representatives in outlying districts, including Kamakura itself; but they did not dominate the country as the previous Shogunate had done. Some feudal lords acquired considerable local influence, and such men never relinquished it. Consequently, there were large areas where the writ of the Ashikaga Shoguns did not run. It was all the more remarkable that the authority of the Ashikaga family should have remained unchallenged for so long. Indeed, the power of families in the strict sense became increasingly important, for loyalty was most effectively preserved within the family unit. As a means of consolidating wealth and property, the old system of distributing patrimony among children was abandoned. A form of primogeniture came to be practised, though the chosen son was not necessarily the eldest, and he could be adopted. From all forms of inheritance women were now excluded.

The death of Go-Daigo did not entail any immediate healing of the breach between the rival Courts. On the contrary, the supporters of Yoshino were successful on two occasions in attacking Kyoto; but after Takauji's death in 1358, the quarrel was patched up, and in 1392 the third Shogun, Yoshimitsu (Takauji's son, Yoshiakira, had tried in vain to expel the Southern Court, as it was called), arrived at an understanding with Yoshino whereby the two lines should again take turns to provide the Emperor. But again it did not work for long, and for this the Ashikaga were responsible. Although Go-Daigo's line still had its partisans, it slowly faded out.

The era when the two Courts were united is called by Japanese historians the Muromachi period, after the quarter in Kyoto where the Shoguns lived. This period was a great age of cultural advance, and it was then that Zen Buddhism achieved its apogee. Zen monks came to wield temporal power; some became diplomats and states-men, proving themselves especially useful in diplomatic exchanges with Korea and China.

Japanese pirates or *wakō* still operated along the China coast, as off Korea, and the Ming Emperors made every effort to bring this menace to an end. Finally, Yoshimitsu, who had united the two Courts, agreed to maintain tributary relations with the third Ming emperor. Every ten years, two ships were to go to China. The mission, several hundred strong, was to carry means of identification in the form of tallies: that is to say, the Chinese issued numbered paper forms which had been detached from a book containing stubs. On arrival the mission was to present the forms for checking against the stubs. At first, this system worked well, as it eliminated pirates and unofficial 'missions', though there was a good deal of competition in Japan to secure the Chinese tallies. Between 1404 and 1410, more than the prescribed number of missions were sent, but between 1433 and 1549, eleven Japanese missions arrived at the Chinese Court.

The Ashikaga derived so much profit from these missions that no objection was raised to Japan being regarded by the Chinese as a state subject to the Ming. The subjection was purely nominal, though the Chinese took it more literally, fully intending that Japan should form part of their empire. In due course, the missions included unofficial ones sponsored by monasteries and even single families. In 1469, the Ōuchi family captured an entire returning mission – cargo, tallies, and all. Thereafter the Ōuchi played a great part in the China trade. As to trade with Korea, this was even more active once piracy had been put down, and the Japanese were allowed to use ports in Korea as settlements.

The trade with China came to an end about the time of the collapse of the Ashikaga Shogunate, though the cessation of commerce was due to a quarrel within the Ōuchi family itself. Meanwhile, domestic trade had made much progress. Although the feudal lords tended to despise the rising merchant class, and did their best to extract profit by taxing goods in their territory, the merchants, conscious of their strength, countered these moves by the formation of guilds. Associations of this nature, or *Za*, had existed for some time; but it was during the Ashikaga Shogunate that they came to prominence. Thus the merchants acquired an identity as a class which they had never previously enjoyed. Just as some of the *Za* had originally been formed under the auspices of shrines and temples, so the religious foundations began to establish dependent institutions, which, patronized increasingly by pilgrims, formed the nucleus of small towns. In other places, such as ports or markets, economic centres grew up independently of religious institutions. Meanwhile, the feudal lords, acting in defence of themselves and their vassals, began to erect huge fortresses; and round these castles, mostly dating from the sixteenth century, towns grew up or proliferated, until every town of any size had its castle, and every castle was surrounded by a growing city. Many of these castle-towns assumed an independence of the central government reflecting the autonomy of the feudal lord. Some were to become the 'capitals' of provinces. As for the castles themselves, they were so well built and so aesthetically satisfying as to ensure their preservation into the industrial and technological age; and when many of them were destroyed in the last war, the government, ignoring the great expense, did not hesitate to reconstruct them. Today, like the castles of England and the châteaux of France, they are largely tourist attractions; but as the feudal age lasted much longer in Japan than in the West, they never fell into ruin, and we can today view them as they were, great buoyant structures dominating the countryside.

The Ashikaga Shogunate, without doubt one of the most 'creative' periods in Japanese history, began to collapse as the result of a bitter struggle called the Ōnin War. (Like other wars, the name was taken from that of the 'year period'.) It was a quarrel regarding succession within the Shogunate; and as it settled nothing, it brought the Ashikaga period to a close in a certain amount of ignominy. Hoping to secure spoil, many feudal lords joined in, and by doing so pulled down the whole edifice of central government. Appropriately, the conflict was also called that of the 'warring states'. Power inevitably went to those who could acquire it, and this meant the more enterprising *daimyo*. Such men became virtual dictators, wielding absolute power over their vassals and retainers, and living off the toil of their peasants. The latter, taxed to the limit and obliged in addition to perform military service, suffered greater oppression as a class than the merchants who were by status subordinate to them. Slowly the *daimyo* began to absorb the old estates, including those nominally owned by the Imperial family and the Kyoto nobles. This led to the increasing impoverishment of the Court and the aristocracy. As a result, some Emperors were not even properly crowned, as the ceremony was too expensive; and the Court could no longer maintain 'retired' emperors. Modern diplomats, invited to the Imperial Palace at the New Year to bow before the Emperor, are given very simple refreshments, which are wrapped up in napkins by the palace staff for consumption at home. This is in commemoration of the time when the Emperor, through poverty, was unable to entertain his guests with the customary munificence.

Hitherto wars, especially those involving family rivalries, had been in the nature of aristocratic games. Now the knight on horseback, though still important, was no longer the typical warrior. Foot-soldiers had become essential elements in the army of the feudal lord. The result was a partial democratization of the armed forces. The Feudal Age, in one aspect, was passing. One sign of the times was the fact that men of lowly birth could advance in society. Even if this did not happen very often, it had never happened previously. Another sign of the times was the banding together of commoners, especially in the rural areas, for the redress of grievances, usually those involving complaints against extortionate usurers. From time to time there were riots and attacks upon storehouses or the offices of money-lenders. Alarmed at the popular unrest, the Shogunate would publish edicts cancelling debts. Such edicts, or acts of 'virtuous administration', had been issued during the Kamakura period; but at that time the nobles were the chief beneficiaries, whereas now it was the common people. Turbulence was likewise created by religious bodies such as the followers of Nichiren and of the True Sect (Jōdo Shinshū). These bodies on occasion 'took over' whole provinces, as when the True Sect ousted the feudal lord of Kaga in 1488, and maintained their authority there for the best part of a century. Often, the Shinshū and the followers of Nichiren came to blows. Near Sakai, which had developed into something like a free city, the True Sect set up a temple-fortress, the Honganji. This was one of the most striking examples of a fortress which became the nucleus of a city; for the city to grow up round the Honganji was Osaka.

To suppose that feudalism in Japan ever assumed a balanced and symmetrical pattern, even during the early Kamakura Shogunate, would be inaccurate. It is equally inaccurate to suppose that the feudal system disappeared when the Ashikaga Shoguns lost their control. In one sense, feudalism lasted in Japan until 1868. Since modern Japan is much nearer to her feudal past than any European nation, certain feudal attitudes, such as paternalism, are still widespread. The assumption is sometimes made that this prolongation of feudalism marked a 'backward' strain in Japanese history, as if she had not 'caught up' with modern nations. This is to judge the world by European standards; for if the rise of nationalism and the outbreak of religious wars of unexampled ferocity are assumed to represent a norm by which other countries should be judged, we are taking a strange view of normality.

4   First contacts with the West

IN RETROSPECT, it is easy to see how Japan, with its central authority temporarily gone, was ripe at the end of the sixteenth century for reunification by other means; but at the time it must have seemed that the country was to be permanently split up into competing principalities. As so often, the new development was brought about, in part at least, by occurrences which were wholly unexpected. These were in the field of commerce. Trade with Korea and China was normal; with countries farther away contact was necessarily sporadic; but with Europe there was no contact at all, until Western seafarers had devised the kind of ship which could keep to the sea for months at a time. The first to achieve this were the Portuguese.

The first Portuguese contact with Japan was accidental. A Chinese junk, carrying three Portuguese, was wrecked on an island off Kyushu in about 1542. The foreigners possessed muskets, which excited such interest in the Japanese that they at once set about copying them. On returning to China, the Portuguese were naturally full of their newly-discovered country, for it had seemed in many ways to be highly civilized. A year or perhaps two years later, Portuguese ships set out to gain ports in Kyushu, hoping to initiate commercial relations. In 1549, however, a Jesuit, Francis Xavier, sailing in a pirate ship from Malacca, arrived in Kagoshima. This was to mark the beginning of a new era for Japan.

Xavier was well received. So indeed were later missionaries, though only six had arrived in Japan by 1560. Perhaps this good reception was due to the fact that the traders were observed to think highly of the missionary colleagues whom they accompanied. Xavier visited Hirado, Yamaguchi, and later Kyoto. At Kyoto, he found a strange situation. The 'king' lived in total seclusion, while the power was in the hands of a military man (absent at the time of Xavier's visit). Unable to contact those in authority, Xavier returned to Yamaguchi, where there is today a church commemorating his stay. At the invitation of the *daimyo*, he then visited Funai. The *daimyo*, Ōtomo Sōrin, the Lord of Bungo, was impressed by Xavier and later himself became a Christian. From Ōtomo, Xavier took a mission back to Goa. This was in 1551.

In a letter addressed from Japan to his fellow-Jesuits at Goa, Xavier described the Japanese people as honest, frugal, dignified, and above all men of honour. Between the lines of this interesting document, we seem to detect an air of puzzlement that such people, though pagans, should display virtue and high-mindedness to so high a degree. Xavier had great trouble with the language, and he was hard put to it to understand certain features of Buddhism, though he engaged in a number of disputations with Buddhist priests. Nevertheless, he had no little success in his missionizing, and he left behind about 1,000 converts. Of the Japanese people he thereafter could not speak too highly. He called them 'the delight of his heart'.

Xavier's deep affection for the Japanese was shared in large part by the merchants. And the merchants were welcomed because the Japanese were anxious to do business, especially in the goods which the Portuguese brought them. There is much argument as to whether the Japanese, beginning with some *daimyo*, embraced Christianity out of pure religious zeal or because it seemed likely to profit them. That many were genuine converts was obvious from the martyrs they made. Many were undoubtedly impelled by the prospect of material gain. There was a third, and possibly the largest, category, which was attracted primarily to the 'way of life' of the Europeans.

We need not exaggerate the differences between Christian and Buddhist doctrine as they appeared to the Japanese. To some, the Christian teaching seemed to be another and more esoteric form of Buddhism, just as the Christian priests appeared to be 'holy men' comparable in dignity and scholarship with some of the Buddhist monks, particularly those of the Zen sect. Nevertheless, many Buddhists saw the Christians as dangerous rivals; and the evident success of the missionaries angered them. Statistics are hard to come by; but by 1600 the number of converts in Japan was probably as many as 300,000, and by 1615 half a million. The Jesuits never achieved such success in the mission field – not even in South America – as they did in Japan.

One reason for the initial tolerance of Christianity was that the Portuguese, with their new techniques and products, seemed to represent a superior civilization. The Japanese are as a race highly sensitive to the achievements of others. This has earned them the reputation of being ingenious imitators. The remarkable fact is that this desire to imitate is matched by a desire no less strong to emulate, and to devise what in time is seen to be wholly original. Secondly, the Japanese have a way of borrowing techniques and methods from abroad as a way of protecting their own traditions. It was to guard their way of life that the Japanese adopted Western methods of defence. Finally, the Japanese have always been intensely curious about other people's beliefs, nor have they found anything incongruous in accepting several forms of belief at the same time. On the other hand, they insist that the essence of an alien belief should be understood in terms of their own outlook on life. Francis Xavier soon perceived this, whereas some of his fellow missionaries failed to do so.

Although the arrival of the foreigners was a stimulus to the Japanese to sink their internal differences, the reunification of Japan was the work of men of outstanding native ability who built upon each other's achievements. The first of these extraordinary men was Nobunaga Oda, born in 1534, a *daimyo* in the area now dominated by Nagoya. He possessed an instinct for power; for he soon began to threaten the authority of other *daimyo* in the neighbourhood, though he also sought to acquire influence through arranging marriage-alliances. Having achieved a good deal of success by these two methods, he became ambitious enough to interfere with politics in the capital. He backed a particular candidate for the Shogunate, and thereupon attacked Kyoto, which he captured in 1568. He found his candidate unsatisfactory, and in 1573 he turned him out. This was the formal end of the Ashikaga Shogunate, for Nobunaga left the position of Shogun vacant. Although he never assumed the title himself, he was without doubt the most powerful military ruler in the country. All his life he remained loyal to the Imperial Court.

Nobunaga's career was one of ceaseless struggle. His most bitter campaigns were those launched against the Buddhist sects which had themselves acquired military power. On Mount Hiei, the Tendai sect had established at least 3,000 monasteries. These Nobunaga destroyed, massacring many of the monks. He also made war upon the True

Sect, though he took ten years to reduce them. This was the end of militant Buddhism. Perhaps it was his hostility to the sects that made him tend to encourage the Christians. Certainly, the latter found in this warrior an unexpectedly benign protector.

Despite his great energy and military success, Nobunaga did not subdue much more than the area of the capital. Another successful commander, Tokugawa Ieyasu, a *daimyo* of about the same status as Nobunaga, entered into alliance with him. Ieyasu also fought the True Sect, and conducted campaigns against neighbouring *daimyo*. Without his aid, Nobunaga would never have been able to consolidate his hold over the capital. Nobunaga had another powerful friend and ally, who was perhaps the most remarkable of the three. Hideyoshi, who had begun as an ordinary foot-soldier, became first his vassal and then Nobunaga's most powerful general, and he it was whom Nobunaga sent to subdue the *daimyo* of West Honshu. This campaign, though increasingly successful, occupied several years; but while Hideyoshi was away, Nobunaga was murdered by another of his vassals (1582). Hideyoshi returned at once to Kyoto and put the rival to death. Nobunaga's grandson, a child, was proclaimed his 'successor', but in due course Hideyoshi personally took over Nobunaga's position. He then began systematically to bring the great *daimyo* under his control, and this included Ieyasu himself, who submitted in 1586. The islands of Shikoku and Kyushu then gave in to him, and finally Hideyoshi marched against the *daimyo* of the Kanto and later of Sendai. This meant that he had acquired control of almost the whole of Japan, for the northernmost island of Hokkaido was still a wild region inhabited by the 'barbarian' Ainu.

Like Nobunaga, Hideyoshi regarded himself, even at the height of his career, as a loyal subject of the Emperor. The Court was now provided for, and the ignominious position of the Emperor and the nobles was alleviated. Both Nobunaga and Hideyoshi acted as ministers at the Court, Hideyoshi being in effect Prime Minister or even Regent. Neither chose to assume the title of Shogun.

Possibly the influence of the Court, but possibly also some inherent feature of the Japanese character, made these two warriors men of taste as well as practical, down-to-earth administrators. They built enormous castles, but they also cultivated the arts. One of Hideyoshi's most lavish entertainments, and possibly one of the greatest ever held, was a Tea Ceremony which he organized at Kyoto in 1587.

This continued for ten days, and many thousand guests attended.

As a ruler, Hideyoshi was a great believer in allowing the *daimyo* autonomy and even exemption from taxation; but he also kept a close eye on them in case they should acquire excessive power. Sometimes he would shift them from one domain to another. This he did with the man whom he knew to be his greatest potential rival, Ieyasu. In Kyushu, where the great Shimazu family, though sub-dued, had been allowed to keep their domain, he set up three more *daimyo* by way of counterbalance: two of these were Christian generals, Konishi and Kuroda, and the third a man known for his hostility to Christianity, Katō Kiyomasa. In order to assist him in his work of governing the country, he appointed a council in Kyoto composed of five persons to whom different spheres of administra-tion were allocated, but who acted together, or in twos or threes, when important decision-making was in question. Like Hideyoshi himself, these were all self-made men.

On the other hand, Hideyoshi was anxious to re-establish the old class distinctions which had been breaking down during the Ashikaga Shogunate, almost as if he wished to prevent others from making the meteoric rise to power which he and some of his followers had achieved. For he was determined to establish a dynasty. He introduced a law forbidding peasants to possess swords, and this he applied very strictly. He also forbade interchange between classes: peasants were not to become merchants, nor were retainers to be allowed to become merchants or farmers. This was the beginning of a social rigidity which was to last for centuries. In practice, by imposing such a system, he was making it easier for the *daimyo* to control their domains.

There was another group towards whom Hideyoshi felt the need to formulate a strict policy, stricter than that of Nobunaga. These were the foreigners, especially the missionaries, and also the Christians among his own people. There was an initial period of tolerance, especially in favour of the merchants, with whom he was anxious to do business; but in 1587, only an hour or two after paying a friendly visit to a Portuguese ship, he changed his mind about the missionaries and decided to expel them all. As to the Christians among the Japanese themselves, he ordered the *daimyo* to cease to impose Christianity on their 'subjects', as some of the Christian lords had done, though he seems not to have minded very much what the ordinary man believed.

46

What prompted Hideyoshi to impose his ban was a growing suspicion that Christianity, as a belief of foreign origin, might undermine the loyalty of the vassals; but he seems to have been willing to await developments, as the ban was not at first strictly enforced. Meanwhile, members of his own entourage were baptized, including some Court ladies. Nevertheless, he observed that some of the Christian *daimyo* had begun to persecute the Buddhists; and this intolerance in a land of religious tolerance, if sectarian strife, shocked him. It is true that some Jesuits were accustomed to breaking Buddhist images. The political motives of the Christian missionaries were underlined when, following the Jesuits, Franciscan missionaries arrived. They eluded the ban of 1587 by acting under the protection of the Spanish embassy from the Philippines, which had arrived first in 1592. Soon Jesuits and Franciscans were at loggerheads, often over questions of trade, and Hideyoshi was confirmed in his belief that missionizing was not always purely religious in intent. In 1597, though ten years after the ban, the blow fell. Hideyoshi crucified a number of Spanish Franciscans, Portuguese Jesuits, and seventeen Japanese Christians. It is said that he had been much influenced by some indiscreet remarks or boastings of a Spanish pilot who had been shipwrecked off the Japan coast in 1596. Certainly, Hideyoshi's attitude had undergone radical change since he had hobnobbed with the Jesuits, especially Father Frois, who knew Japanese well, and with the Jesuit Vice-Provincial. During the latter's much-publicized visit to Japan in 1586, Hideyoshi had given him to understand that, after conquering China, he would declare Christianity the official religion of Japan.

On this same occasion, Hideyoshi disclosed that he intended to invade Korea, presumably as a first step to the more ambitious campaign. He sounded the Vice-Provincial as to whether he might purchase, through him, two Portuguese men-of-war. The attack on Korea came in 1592. Hideyoshi left the fighting to his generals, including Christian ones commanding a Christian army. There were two expeditions, the first of which met with success, though the Korean navy was often more than a match for that of Japan. Following Hideyoshi's instructions, the Japanese endeavoured to win over the Koreans by something akin to propaganda, and they set about integrating the country they had occupied into the Japanese sphere. This enterprise did not succeed: a resistance movement, especially among the farmers, grew up. Nevertheless, the Japanese pushed into Manchuria, and, after a desperate Korean appeal for help to the Chinese, routed the new enemy. An armistice was then declared, after which the Chinese, who had realized the magnitude of the Japanese threat, crossed the Yalu river in great numbers and began to threaten Seoul. A parley then began, with envoys from China arriving in Nagoya and later in Kyoto. Some misunderstandings occurred, because Hideyoshi's generals had discussed terms of which Hideyoshi was unaware. Furious at what he considered to be the arrogant tone of the Chinese envoys, he swore once more to invade China, and in 1597 another force was prepared and dispatched. This time the Chinese were ready to meet it, and a violent battle ensued. The Japanese prevailed, but the Chinese, having retreated, were back the next spring; only to be defeated along with the Koreans by the Japanese once again. In September 1598, however, Hideyoshi died, and another armistice was declared.

Despite their over-all military successes, the Japanese forces had been under considerable pressure, and the result was exhaustion. The idea of conquering China, and even of removing the capital of the new Japanese empire to Peking, had been shown to be a mirage. Centuries later, it was to be revived.

There is evidence that towards the end of his career Hideyoshi suffered from mental strain and instability. He had attempted too much. Yet even though he was Japan's greatest general, it must not be thought that he was merely a coarse, ruthless man of action. One side of him loved the sweet things of life: he had many amorous affairs. It is said that his sudden *volte face* on Christianity was due to the refusal of Christian girls to submit to him. But his letters show that, despite outbursts of cruelty, he had a generous and tender side to his nature, and he was devoted to his natural son, Hideyori, and to his mother, whose death in 1588 reduced him to a paroxysm of grief. He was a devotee of the Noh, and he knew many plays by heart. Judging from the attention he gave to the question of his successor, he seems to have had it in mind to retire after the conquest of China, for he prepared one of his many castles for a life of repose. After his death, there was a bitter quarrel over the succession.

If military gain from the invasion of Korea was slight, there accrued some cultural advantage. The Japanese brought back from Korea printing techniques; and from among the captives there were a number of potters, who exerted great influence upon a craft for which Japan is still famous.

When Hideyoshi died, Hideyori was only five years old. Accordingly, a council of regents was formed to carry on the government; but, as had happened before, one of their number soon began to dominate the rest. This was Tokugawa Ieyasu, who had remained at home when Hideyoshi's generals were in Korea. Other *daimyo* banded together to overthrow Ieyasu; but in due course he defeated them at Sekigahara (1600), not so much as a result of military prowess as because of treachery among his enemies. Following his victory, Ieyasu took as his prize the great castle at Osaka (which he handed over to Hideyori), and set about rewarding those *daimyo* who had supported him. Of the 214 domains, he confiscated 91 outright. In 1603, the Emperor appointed him Shogun; but Ieyasu was apparently anxious neither to flaunt this title nor to settle in Kyoto, so he decided to make his residence Edo, one of his own domains. Here he had built a huge castle. Although officially Shogun, he still paid respect to Hideyori, and he knew that some *daimyo* were ready to support the latter's claims to be the true successor of Hideyoshi. Ieyasu also built Nijō castle in Kyoto, as a means to controlling the local *daimyo*, for he kept a deputy there.

Supporters of Hideyori began to grow in numbers. Many of them were military men, who, following Ieyasu's redistribution of fiefs, found themselves both propertyless and masterless. They were called *rōnin*, a category of warrior who were to play an important part in later history. In the end, Ieyasu realized that he would need to eliminate Hideyori, so he mobilized an army to defeat him. In the ensuing engagement at Osaka in 1614, which was at first indecisive, Ieyasu indulged in more than one act of treachery in order to gain the upper hand. Hideyori then committed suicide, and Ieyasu, having disposed of the only serious rival house to his own, became, like his two predecessors but with far greater effect, supreme ruler of Japan.

In 1605, Ieyasu had renounced the title of Shogun, and his son Hidetada formally succeeded him. Evidently the motive was to ensure that the power, and therefore the title, should remain in the Tokugawa family. And so it did for some two hundred and fifty years.

5 Japan in isolation

IN 1600, AN ENGLISHMAN, Will Adams, had arrived in Japan. He did so on a Dutch vessel, the *Liefde*, of which he was the chief navigator or pilot major. The ship was one of five sent from Holland to do business in competition with the Portuguese and the Spanish. On the voyage, there were frequent storms, and the *Liefde* made Kyushu with great difficulty. It berthed at the island of Hirado. By that time many of the crew had died. Adams and his companions were received in a hostile manner by the Jesuits; but fortunately Ieyasu heard of his arrival and summoned Adams to Osaka. Ieyasu also ordered that the *Liefde* should be stripped of its guns. After keeping Adams waiting for a year, Ieyasu took him into his service. Adams was set to work to build men-of-war; for Ieyasu had realized how badly on the whole the Japanese navy had fared in Korea and how effective were the Portuguese. Not only did Adams show himself an expert at shipbuilding, but his personality impressed Ieyasu, and very soon a friendship developed between the two. Adams became a kind of confidential adviser on matters relating to foreign trade, the political and diplomatic intentions of the Portuguese, Spanish, Dutch and English, and above all on religious matters. He was treated with great generosity, became a landowner, and married a Japanese (though he had a wife at home). He had sought permission to leave Japan after five years' stay, but this plea had been refused.

From Adams, Ieyasu learnt much about the divisions of Christendom, and about the rivalry between Christian nations. This rivalry did not displease him. Although he was anxious to expand Japan's trade he did not want to see the power of any one European nation predominate. Above all, he was riled that his negotiations with the Portuguese traders had to be conducted through the Jesuit missionaries. On this point, Adams enlightened him. Such deference to religious bodies, Adams explained, was unnecessary. Trade could be conducted as a purely secular concern. Ieyasu therefore encouraged the Dutch to trade with Japan, finding to his surprise that this had no religious implications.

For some years Ieyasu conducted trading relations with the European powers with a measure of impartiality. He also allowed missionary activity to continue, and even permitted the Spaniards, with whom he wished to improve relations, to set up a mission in Edo itself. But he was still cautious and suspicious.

In 1614, he openly changed his tactics. He had published two edicts directly against Christianity in 1606 and 1609, but now he proclaimed a law suppressing both the preaching and the practice of the faith. It is said that he was particularly alarmed at the increase of Christian converts among his immediate entourage, whose loyalty he sometimes doubted, and among certain *daimyo;* but he was influenced even more by his observation of the quarrels between the denominations, particularly Protestants and Catholics, let alone the sectarian rivalry between Jesuits and Franciscans, and by his knowledge, obtained through various reports, that in other parts of the world, particularly South America, the Church had been the spearhead of imperial conquest. In point of fact, under Ieyasu's rule, there were no executions, but he died in 1616, and his successor, Hidetada, proved a good deal more ruthless.

The persecution of Christianity in Japan was a sombre episode. Nevertheless, Hidetada's point of view must be understood. To him, the very numerous Japanese converts were the potential allies of an invading power, such as the Spaniards – who were well established in Manila – might become. Neither he nor Ieyasu seems to have entertained any hostility to Christianity as such. Under persecution, the Christians, both foreign and Japanese, displayed often great courage. Of the 156 missionaries in Japan at the time of the 1614 edict, 47 succeeded in evading the authorities; and of those who had left, a number returned in secret. The fortitude of many Japanese converts was such that the Japanese Christian resistance was held up as an example by Catholics in Douai to their persecuted co-religionists in England. There were many recantations; but a Christian 'underground' was formed, especially in the neighbourhood of Nagasaki, and this endured, with family instructing family, until, centuries later, when the practice of Christianity was once more permitted, the faithful came out of hiding.

One of the methods for testing or singling out Christians was to try to induce them to step on a Christian image or crucifix. Curiously enough, verbal recantations had to be made in the name of Christ and the Virgin. What happened to those who refused to abjure their faith in this way, and by signing a sworn affidavit, became more and more atrocious. Yet Christianity endured in a manner which astonished and perplexed the authorities. The climax to the anti-Christian campaign was the Shimabara rebellion in 1637, when the still Christian peasantry, together with some *rōnin*, rose against the feudal lord. There were probably at least 20,000 of them, apart from women and children, and not until an army of 100,000 and a Dutch ship had been brought up to the attack, were they successfully overcome. At the end, they were reduced to fighting with iron cauldrons and pots. All were slaughtered, but the attackers suffered severely too, losing about 13,000 men. This encounter between peasants and a highly-trained samurai army taught a lesson to the Shogun. He had been planning an attack on the Philippines, but this project was now quietly abandoned.

The Shimabara rebellion and its sequel marked the end of overt Christian influence in Japan. From time to time missionaries landed in disguise, but they were one and all rounded up. The practice of 'stepping on the crucifix' was a familiar story outside Japan. It will be remembered that Gulliver, in his brief stay in the country, speaks of it as a common practice.

Although Ieyasu had originally hoped that by removing the Christians he would have a freer hand with foreign trade, his fears of a 'takeover' of Japan induced him to restrict commerce, or at least to keep its activities in his own hands. This applied also to Japanese trade abroad, where silver was exchanged for Chinese silk. European ships were confined to the artificial island of Deshima off Hirado, and to Nagasaki, though the English, who had sent out a mission in 1613, gave it up in 1623. Soon, Japanese were forbidden to go abroad (or if they did so, they were refused re-admission), and ships were restricted in size, so that overseas trade was impossible. The Dutch and Chinese continued to trade at Nagasaki. Otherwise the country was virtually isolated from the world.

The suppression of Christianity marked a triumph for Buddhism, and thereafter Japanese were required to 'register' at their local temple. Even today, many families retain an association with a particular temple, though they may be Buddhist only in name, and may indeed 'visit' the temple only once, that is to say, when their body is brought thither for their funeral rites.

It was during the long Tokugawa Shogunate that the strict division of classes was formally confirmed. At the apex of society was the Emperor, still a venerated if secluded figure, whose regent was the Shogun. Then came the *daimyo*. Under these were the *shi*, the *bushi* or military caste, of which the samurai were a branch;[1] the *nō*, or peasants; the *kō*, or artisans; and the *shō*, or merchants. Each class knew its place, and each owed allegiance in its own manner to the *daimyo*. At the lowest social level, there was another class, the outcasts or *eta*, whose trade was confined to leather goods. Some mystery attaches to these despised people, whose occupation is correspondingly scorned; for although there is now a public conscience about them, and although some *eta* have managed by force of character to rise in the world, there are still today whole villages or districts inhabited by outcasts, to which many Japanese are reluctant to penetrate. One theory is that they are descendants of Korean prisoners.[2]

Notwithstanding the separation of Japan from the rest of the world, the country did not go through a period of stagnation. On the contrary, there was great internal economic expansion. Towns such as Edo, Osaka and Kyoto grew in size. Agricultural productivity increased. Above all, the standard of education was raised. Indeed, it was during the Tokugawa Shogunate that Japan acquired that high level of literacy which she, alone of Oriental nations and in advance of some Western ones, has retained. Without doubt, much of the progress of Japan, which was otherwise slowed down during the period, especially in the technological sphere, was due to the fact that almost all Japanese were not merely literate but highly so. Literacy in the West tends to imply a minimum knowledge of reading and writing, with an expected low standard in the latter accomplishment: whereas a literate Japanese is one who knows a large number of *characters*, some of great complication, which on the whole he can handle well.

A development of importance in the cultural sphere at this time was the re-emphasis upon the teachings of Confucius. The Confucian philosophy had penetrated from China through Korea very early. There are signs of it in the Constitution, or set of precepts, addressed to the ruling classes of Japan by Shōtoku Taishi; [3] and in the eighth century, it was taught in schools, special emphasis being placed on filial piety. Confucianism is essentially an ethical doctrine. So far as we can tell, Confucius himself, who lived in the sixth century BC, was a devout man, believing in a Supreme Being or *T'ien*, which means Heaven; but what he chiefly sought to do, in a disordered world, was to preach the advantages of good, stable, but not harsh government, based on family loyalties. There is a story that, in the course of his wanderings in exile, Confucius came upon a solitary woman weeping. Asked the reason for her grief, she replied that at that spot she had recently buried her father-in-law, her husband and her son, all of whom had been attacked by tigers. When Confucius enquired why the family had decided to settle in so dangerous a place, the woman answered: 'There is no oppressive government here.' Turning to his companions, Confucius remarked: 'Take note of this. Oppressive government is fiercer than a tiger.'

That the Confucian ethic should have found a ready welcome in seventeenth-century Japan was no doubt due to its being in essential harmony with the Tokugawa social system; for the ethic, with its emphasis upon contentment with one's lot and with the place in society in which one was born, enjoined loyalty to the government which held the hierarchical order together. The tiger of despotism was to be preferred to that of anarchy. This is perhaps why Confucius has made an appeal to certain intellectuals favouring totalitarian regimes. Moreover, the reverence for parents and for ancestors, as preached by Confucius, was fully compatible with Shintō doctrine, which also underwent a revival at this time, though for other reasons it came into conflict with the Confucian movement. As for Buddhism, its other-worldly side served to complement the injunction to be content with one's lot, since any injustice experienced in the present life was part of that 'illusion' from which Nirvana would deliver unhappy mortals. It is not an accident, therefore, that the Confucian teaching should have been re-introduced chiefly by Zen priests, notably by Fujiwara Seika (1561–1619), almost as if to confirm the point that larges doses of Zen need to be counteracted by a physic which lends the character an added stability.

A further contribution made by Confucianism, to which the samurai found themselves especially attuned, was the work of more orthodox scholars, particularly Yamaga Sokō (1622-85). It was Yamaga who first explicitly formulated the samurai ideal or 'the way of the warrior'. Another name for this was *Bushido* (i.e., military code). The term signifies chivalry in its Japanese form; but although the two terms are by no means synonymous, *Bushido* stands for honourable behaviour, especially to a conquered enemy, though today it has a somewhat old-fashioned ring. Japanese of samurai connections are always proud of the fact; but in practice the samurai ideal sometimes permitted conduct of startling callousness, as when an insult or supposed affront, especially from an inferior or a foreigner, was avenged by summary killing. This was called *kirisute*, literally 'to cut down and leave'.

In the Japanese army, the samurai came to fill the gap between the old feudal conscription and the modern system of conscription, which was introduced in 1874. In essence, however, the samurai followed a way of life; and this acquired such reputation and prestige that popular legends soon grew up round it, the influence of which still prevails among the public. Just as he had two swords, a long and a short, the samurai had two names, a family name and a personal one. The practice of carrying two swords caused the left shoulder to be lower than the right. The samurai ideal was followed by women too. They were taught to use the *naginata*, or long spear with curved blade, and also the *kama*, or curved dagger; and there are many stories, some authentic, of the bravery of samurai women both in self-defence and in support of their menfolk.

Although the teaching of Confucius was to lose some of its vogue, it played so important a part in the formation of the Japanese tradition that modern Japanese society is still subtly affected by it. Like the Puritan tradition in Britain and America, it has provoked its own reaction, but a modicum of it is still there to be reacted against. Above all, the average Japanese still tends to regard society as a permanently established order, to which it is his duty to conform, in contrast to the Western view that man's duty is to detach himself from society, and, if possible, to 'make good' or 'distinguish' himself. Reverence for the old is another marked Japanese character-istic, and this owes much to Confucius's teaching concerning filial piety. Elderly Japanese, especially men, do not feel that life has passed them by, or that they are permanently excluded from its pleasures, as the not uncommon sight of bar-hostesses cuddling elderly gentlemen vividly attests: conduct which, if Confucius might not have approved, his doctrine may have helped to promote.

In consequence of the development of education during the Tokugawa Shogunate, the merchant class in particular evolved its own cultural interests, and some of the most typical Japanese art and literature was produced during this period.[4] There was the work of the 'Japanese Shakespeare', Chikamatsu (1653-1724), especially in the field of puppet drama or *bunraku*, though Chikamatsu's plays were included in the repertory of another and more popular dramatic form, *kabuki*. Indeed, the latter was perhaps the most typical form of entertainment of the rising middle class, and there is still an enthusiastic public for it today. To the Western eye, the acting of *kabuki* is decidedly 'ham'; but the Japanese audience derives enormous pleasure from certain stylized modes of presentation, and it will greet these with wild applause and appropriate comments. The actors are all men; and, as with Noh, there is a tradition for son to succeed father, and for a famous 'acting name' to be conferred upon a worthy successor. The plays themselves contain a marked element of melodrama, and not a little violence: to this extent *kabuki* expresses a range of emotions totally different from the Noh. Whereas the Noh would seem to have provided a mental relief for the warrior class, *kabuki* appealed to a bourgeoisie which, enjoying a comparatively sheltered life, needed its thirst for action to be satisfied in the imaginative sphere.

During this same period, two other art forms were brought to perfection. One was *haiku* and the other *ukiyo-e*. The Occident has no precise equivalent to either: both are quintessentially Japanese. *Haiku* are poems of 17 syllables, disposed in lines of 5, 7 and 5 syllables, and expressing an image or idea related to the season or to the change of seasons. Characterized by a delicacy hard to render in translation, their beauty in the original can be described only faintly by the foreigner; but even so, the magic can on occasion be conveyed:

> A fallen flower
> Returning to the branch?
> It was a butterfly.[5]

The most famous author of *haiku*, in its traditional form, was the poet Bashō (1644-94), whose productions in this *genre* reached a degree of refinement beyond which, in the opinion of many Japanese, it is impossible to go. On the other hand, the number of *haiku* written since Bashō's day, and produced by every class of Japanese from the Emperor and Empress downwards, must run into many thousands. *Haiku* competitions are held annually; there can be few Japanese who have not written some. Self-expression in this miniature form would seem to be a psychological necessity. Many *haiku* are wistful and nostalgic in tone, reflecting a view of life akin to that preached by Buddhism; but the emphasis on nature – there are no *haiku* written about industry or technology, for example[6] – suggests the pervasive influence of Shintō.

Woodblock prints, or *ukiyo-e*, which reached their zenith in the work of Hokusai and Hiroshige, both artists belonging to the nineteenth century, reflect again the Japanese preoccupation with the passing moment. Many examples of *ukiyo-e* depict what the Japanese call 'the floating world', which is the meaning of the word *ukiyo*. This world embraces both delicate landscapes and the life of the pleasure quarters, especially those of Edo. Just as the Japanese love of cherry blossom is due chiefly to the fact that the delicate blossoms last for so short a time, so the experience of pleasure is fugitive. Both thus serve to remind the participant or the spectator of the impermanence of things. There is still much interest in *ukiyo-e*, and exhibitions of modern work are regularly organized.

If an account were to be given of European people during this same period, it would refer to poetry and art chiefly as cultivated by the so-called intelligentsia. In the case of Japan, aesthetic interests are much more socially pervasive. This is due both to the literacy of the Japanese in the broad sense, and to their psychological make-up. They require beauty and delicacy in everyday life in a manner hardly conceivable to the Westerner: few people would think of placing examples of flower-arrangement in the privy.[7] On the other hand, the Japanese devotion to art is not necessarily separated, as it so often is in the West, from other interests: it is part of their whole philosophy of life. When a Japanese sits down to writing, he composes the characters as accurately and elegantly as he can. It is impossible for them to be 'badly written' out of individual caprice, as 'bad writing' is tolerantly allowed of the Westerner. In other words, when a Japanese child learns to read and write, he is learning not merely his 'letters', but his art and indeed his entire *Weltan-*

schauung. Semantics, aesthetics and metaphysics are absorbed to-gether. Naturally, this is not always a conscious process.[8]

Hence perhaps the reluctance of the Japanese to betray the 'secrets' of their culture, though this may be due to an incapacity to abstract one attitude from the whole. To take an up-to-date example. As an academic subject, philosophy is taught in Japan, and there is not merely much interest in Western thought, but a good deal of philosophy written in the Western manner; but one cannot help feeling that the Japanese no more believe in academic theories than they believe in some of the findings of Western psychology. It is doubtful enough whether Western thinkers, let alone laymen, really believe in the philosophy of Locke, Kant or Hegel; they merely entertain and analyse the ideas propounded by these men. Although some Japanese have mastered Western thought, and have even taught it to Europeans, it is still more doubtful whether they believe, in their heart of hearts, that the world is like the picture of it given by the great European masters. The Japanese derive their view of life from something other than 'systems of thought'; and in so far as this is the case, their ability to elaborate or expound a rational 'point of view' is limited. As Basil Hall Chamberlain says in his *Things Japanese*, 'although the word "philosophy" can be found in Japanese dictio-naries, the thing itself is scarcely Japanese.' Thus although the Japanese attitude to life bears some resemblance to that of the French, the Gallic addiction to abstract reasoning is something wholly foreign to the Japanese mentality.

The emphasis on good taste, hard as that quality may be to define, is no doubt responsible for the absence in Japanese literature and art of a coarseness which in the West is never far below the surface. True, an erotic tradition exists in Japan; but, apart from commercial pornography, it did not erupt into literature until the Japanese began to undergo the influence of certain Western writers. The erotic prints, of which so much is heard, were intended for the limited market always existing for such things, though sometimes they were used for sexual education, especially of girls about to be married. Similarly, what we learn of the life of the 'gay quarters', such as the great Yoshiwara district of Edo (roughly the area covered by present-day Asakusa), suggests the absence of debauchery in the cruder sense.

Some works on Japan, including Sir George Sansom's admirable

Short Cultural History, tend to give the impression that the life of the commoners at this time, especially during the so-called Genroku period (1688-1703), was of an extreme dissoluteness: but Sansom goes on to point out that, compared with 'the industrious millions of peasants', the townspeople were few in number, and that the more licentious books and pictures portrayed the citizens' 'more extravagant' amusements.[9]

The novels of Saikaku (1642-93), though as moralistic at root as the plays of Chikamatsu, could be on occasion erotic, and those of his followers more so; but the Japanese do not react to the erotic as we do in the West – that is, by first suppressing it and then, in the name of 'freedom of expression', by flooding the market with it. In general, their attitude is more balanced.

Although it is accurate to speak of the 'industrious millions of peasantry', the position of this class was by no means easy. Some farmers enjoyed a robust and affluent life, as their strong and commodious houses testify to this day; but the majority lived under conditions of great severity. Although they were the class which grew the nation's sacred food, they suffered ruthless taxation, sometimes up to 40 or 50 per cent of their rice product. Indeed, agriculture was the chief source of government revenue. If there were a bad harvest, the position of the farmers could be desperate. Dating from early times, there are records of the extreme measures adopted by the peasants to secure even a bare subsistence. One of the most common was the sale of girl-children to professional child-brokers. It must not be assumed, however, that this practice meant inevitable degradation, or even that it was confined to times of stress. Some brokers acted exclusively for city geisha-houses; and apart from the fair sum of money (perhaps £50 or £60 in modern terms) which the farmer would receive, the girl would thereafter undergo a prolonged, if strict, training, and be assured of good food and fine clothes for a period of years and perhaps for life, with the chance of a good marriage into the bargain. No wonder that with such advantages in view, the family would not always await the onset of material disaster. Although such glamorous careers must have been rare, we know from records that, whatever the girl may personally have thought of her prospects on such occasions, her village companions considered her fortunate enough to deserve a ceremonial farewell. They also fêted her return, if her employer kept his side of the contract. When recruits for geisha-houses were much in demand, the villages were regularly scoured for suitable trainees; but some of these brokers, whatever they might claim, were concerned to supply houses of prostitution. And although a form of contract may have been entered into in such cases, it was in practice rarely honoured, and it was regarded as void if the girl got into debt. Finally, there would be cases in which the child, perhaps a baby, was sold to a broker cash down, with no questions asked. Such children were often simply done away with.

Although these practices may have prevented many country families from sinking into penury, or dying of starvation, there were always people who sought to bring about their cessation. On more than one occasion, however, a charitable organization, endeavouring to rescue a child from the broker, would meet with opposition from the family itself. This was partly the result of ignorance or stupidity, but partly from a deep-rooted feeling that a girl-child was of lesser value than a boy, and that it was the girl's duty, assuming she was old enough to understand such an ethical point, to sacrifice herself for her family's good.

Some idea of the contempt in which the peasants were held by their overlords may be gained by the tone of certain edicts issued at about this time. One dated 1649 read: 'Peasants are people without sense or forethought. Therefore they must not give rice to their children at harvest time, but must save food for the future. They should eat millet, vegetables, and other coarse food instead of rice.'[10] Or again: 'If [the edict forbidding quarrelling] is disobeyed, both sides will be put to death, without enquiry into right or wrong.'[11] Promulgated originally in the fifteenth century, this edict suggests a condition in which the authorities had reason to fear disruption in social life, and were determined to ensure good order at any price; and the same fear prevailed throughout the Tokugawa Shogunate. Yet it was one thing to forbid on pain of death disputes between individuals; it was another to prevent peasants from banding together and venting their wrath against an oppressive feudal lord or government. Under the Tokugawas, the number of peasant rebellions exceeded one thousand; and of the petitions presented during this period, more than half were judged in favour of the peasants – a sign that oppression could be tempered with justice.

Having effectively sealed Japan off from outside, and having forbidden movement within Japan except under authorization, the Tokugawas brought into being a social system which was as near to being static as possible. Depending on a man's status his living-quarters, his dress, and the degree to which he had to do honour to his superiors were all meticulously prescribed. No modern society has ever reached such a degree of 'immobility'.

Centralized control was exercised through the *daimyo*, in whose domains, or *han*, the Shogun did not as a rule interfere. A *han* was measured according to the amount of taxable rice it was able to produce. At the beginning of the Tokugawa era, the country was divided into 295 *han*, though this number was later reduced. Not merely a contribution of rice but military service was required of each domain.

Given this measure of independence among his vassals, the Shogun's constant preoccupation was how to keep the *daimyo* themselves under control. This was done through a variety of expedients. As had happened between the Shoguns and the Imperial family, the establishment of marriage-ties between the Tokugawas and the families of the *daimyo* became a useful method of ensuring loyalty, whereas such alliances among the *daimyo* themselves were discouraged. The most effective way of ensuring subservience, however, was by the method of hostages: that is to say, the Shogun would order every *daimyo* to leave his wife and children at Edo for a prescribed period. There was also a system called *sankin kōtai*, or 'alternate attendance', whereby the lord himself was obliged to attend the Shogun's court annually to do homage. The hostage system began as a voluntary act signifying trust, but in 1634 it became compulsory. The system of 'alternate attendance', which also began as a voluntary gesture, was legally continued by edicts issued in 1633 and 1642. Much of the traffic making for Edo went along the famous Tōkaidō highway, beginning in Kyoto; and there were special posts not far from Edo, here and on other routes, at which all those coming and going were carefully scrutinized. A particular look-out was made for women leaving Edo, as this might indicate the engineering of plans hostile to the government. At Edo itself, the establishments of the *daimyo* were subject to strict regulation. The *daimyo* were graded in importance, and their military strength carefully controlled, as was the number of their retinue.

Given that half the *daimyo* were in attendance at Edo at a time, together with the families of the other half, the Shogun was able to maintain a grip on his people which ensured his supreme power. Naturally, the expense of maintaining establishments at Edo was considerable, especially as many of the houses were luxurious. A large proportion of a *daimyo*'s income went to provide for these second homes, and the financial burden eventually became very heavy. Moreover, some of the richer *daimyo* maintained more than one house in Edo. This was true of the most powerful of all the *daimyo*, Maeda, whose retinue ran into thousands. Although the system of 'alternate attendance' and of hostages kept the *daimyo* relatively weak, the result of this regular convergence on the capital was stimulating for 'society', and it lent to the life of Edo a glamour such as few capitals possessed. Woodblock prints of the time convey something of this colour and vitality, which was enhanced by the almost continuous ceremonial. Moreover, the constant progress back and forth of armed and bannered processions kept an otherwise 'static' social system in constant movement. Inns along the prescribed routes did a flourishing trade, and the official roads were well maintained.

The super-*daimyo* were naturally the Tokugawas themselves. Their property, concentrated mostly round Edo but including the large towns and the gold and silver mines of remote Sado Island off the Japan Sea coast, was several times the size of the Maeda domains. And their personal retinue was correspondingly large. Although they formed a Court in themselves, they continued to act as if they held authority from the Imperial Court at Kyoto, and this they provided with a generous income. At the same time, they kept a close eye on the Emperor and his nobles, even regulating details of the ceremonial. This was done through a Shogunal deputy, who, in addition to his responsibilities in this sphere, acted as military governor of Kyoto.

The Tokugawas had revived the *Bakufu* (see p. 28), and this form of government branched out from the system under which the Tokugawa family had ruled itself. There were a variety of committees, both advisory and executive, and a number of commissioners who supervised temples and shrines (though only in their secular aspect), economic questions, matters of censorship and intelligence, and justice. Legal affairs and regulations were highly complicated, but they were summed up in codes called 'Laws for the Military Houses', the list of which had been proclaimed by Ieyasu. At the peasant level, minor disputes were settled locally according to established custom. In the case of matters deemed by the Shogun to be of supreme national importance, posters or notices were displayed in conspicuous places. This applied in particular to the ban on Christianity.

Both the samurai code and the Confucian ethic, though affecting the upper class, influenced society as a whole. There can have been few societies in which an *ethical*, as opposed to a religious, system pervaded all classes; but this was undoubtedly due in part to the spread of literacy. Whatever the immobility of society in the Tokugawa era, there was no *cultural* stagnation. 'Dutch learning' *(rangaku)*, however inadequate, meant that books circulated throughout the country. 'Enquiry was free, and the expression of opinion nearly so – except for a ban on Christianity.' [12] Thus the ordinary Japanese was influenced by the manners of the samurai, who, gradually renouncing their habitual contempt for learning, began to form something like an intelligentsia. Their code of manners attained a prestige which might otherwise have characterized merely their own dealings among themselves. Certain principles of conduct pervaded society, and their influence is today by no means extinct, such as those referred to in Chapter 1 – *giri*, duty, and *on*, indebtedness, or the debt of gratitude owed to someone who has done a kindness or rendered a service. The strict application of these principles in the smallest affairs of life made for social cohesion and smoothness in communities which were already tightly knit, though it also made for a certain artificiality of conduct. On the other hand, when Japan was opened up again, the Japanese people were a disciplined body capable of coping, as others might not have been, with pressures and challenges of a wholly new kind.

Even so, it would not be true to say that the Tokugawa period was one of abiding peace. There were a few attempted *coups d'état*, but nothing, until the end, in the shape of a rebellion. In fact, before the events leading to the Meiji Restoration, the only major revolt in Japan was the Shimabara Rebellion, unless we include the Ainu revolt in Hokkaido in 1669, which was put down by the *daimyo* of Matsumae; but Hokkaido was hardly as yet a part of the Japanese community. The most disaffected element of the nation were the *rōnin*. These masterless men were still causing trouble, and in 1651 they even tried to stage their own *coup d'état*. It failed. Of all their exploits, however, the most famous and that which has fired the popular imagination to this day, was the episode of the 'forty-seven *rōnin*'.

The bare account of the event hardly suffices to explain its potency. In 1703, a *daimyo* from West Honshu had been provoked to draw his sword in the Shogun's castle at Edo. As this gesture amounted to a crime, the *daimyo* was ordered by the Shogunate to commit suicide, after which his *han* was seized. Forty-seven of his samurai retainers, becoming *rōnin*, decided to revenge themselves upon the official responsible for the trouble. For a period of two years they lay low, some even deserting their families, for they feared that their intentions might become known. Then one night they assembled together, and, entering the house of the offending official, killed him. Having taken their revenge, they had no alternative but to commit suicide by *seppuku* (hara-kiri) in their turn. This act, and the reason for it, has virtually immortalized the forty-seven *rōnin*, for they are held to have embodied to perfection the feudal ideal of loyalty; and the fact that their story is still retold today in drama and film, and their tomb in Tokyo at the Sengakuji temple visited by thousands, shows the esteem in which this virtue is still held.[13]

Although it must have seemed to the early Tokugawa Shoguns that they had built a social system almost impervious to change, the system gradually began to break down, chiefly for financial reasons. The expenditure of the *daimyo* soon came to be beyond all but the most wealthy among them, and the *Bakufu* also found itself in financial difficulties. The yield of rice proved insufficient for a growing population (there were about 30 million Japanese in 1721), and there were no imports to meet the difference. Hence the periodic peasant revolts. Some attempt to reform was made, especially by the eighth Shogun, Yoshimune, who, among other measures to curb expenditure, cut down the time which *daimyo* were required to stay in Edo. But what Yoshimune saved on the one hand he lost on the other. He taxed the peasants even more heavily than before, and he limited the foreign trade still being carried on in Nagasaki. The stipends of the retainers were reduced; and since these were now paid in rice, the yield in money of that portion which they were obliged to sell proved insufficient to meet their basic expenses.

Another administrator, Tanuma, did his best to promote production, especially in the field of mining; but he incurred unpopularity;

and he was said, perhaps unjustly, to have encouraged bribery and corruption. He was followed by Matsudaira Sadanobu, who endeavoured to restore the old feudal virtues. In order to combat the effects of recurrent famine, he set about establishing a chain of storehouses. He also introduced sumptuary laws, and cut down government expenditure.

Finally, bringing us into the nineteenth century, Mizuno Tadakuni made a further heroic effort to restore feudal conditions. He ordered farmers who had migrated to the towns to return to their farms, thereby seeking to ensure compliance with an old regulation. He, too, drastically curtailed government spending. In support of the Confucian ethical code, he enjoined the virtues of plain living and thrift. But such panic conservatism was too late, and out of touch with social changes. For, despite the discontent of the farmers and the lack of technical means, agriculture had made some progress. No situation could have been more unsuitable, at least at the psychological level, to meet a threat which, over those long years of isolation, had always hung over far-seeing statesmen. This came, as before, from outside.

6   Opening up to the West

THE APPEARANCE of the 'Black Ships' in 1858 was not, so to speak, a sudden and unexpected intrusion. 'Dutch Learning' had sufficiently penetrated the country to make the more literate of the samurai aware in some degree of what was going on in the outside world. Although there was a school of so-called 'National Learning' *(koku-gaku)*, which was anti-Confucian and based on a revived Shintō, and although thinkers such as Hirata Atsutane (1776-1843) preached that Japan was a land of the gods, there were men of a different outlook, such as Hiraga Gennai (1728-79) and Honda Toshiaki (1744-1821), who openly defended Western methods, in so far as they were acquainted with them. Honda even went so far as to suggest that Japan should become the 'England of the East' and embark upon imperial conquest. He also advocated the abolition of the Chinese character and the adoption of the Western alphabet: a recurrent recommendation. Then there were *daimyo* and even Shoguns who took an interest in Western science, not least medicine. Dutch books were translated or laboriously copied and furtively circulated. Sometimes reformers were silenced, and even put to death; but the Achilles' heel of Nagasaki made it impossible to keep the new ideas out.

As European maritime initiative grew, so more ships were wrecked on Japan's shores. Some, though not all, of the sailors were badly treated, and the powers began to contemplate making a new approach to the Japanese authorities. In 1845, an American in command of two warships entered Edo Bay. He had orders from Washington to seek the opening of trade negotiations. The *Bakufu* refused to consider the request. Then in 1853, Commodore Perry arrived. He brought with him a letter from the President of the United States, asking both for the 'opening up' of Japan and for fair treatment for American sailors.

Map of Japan

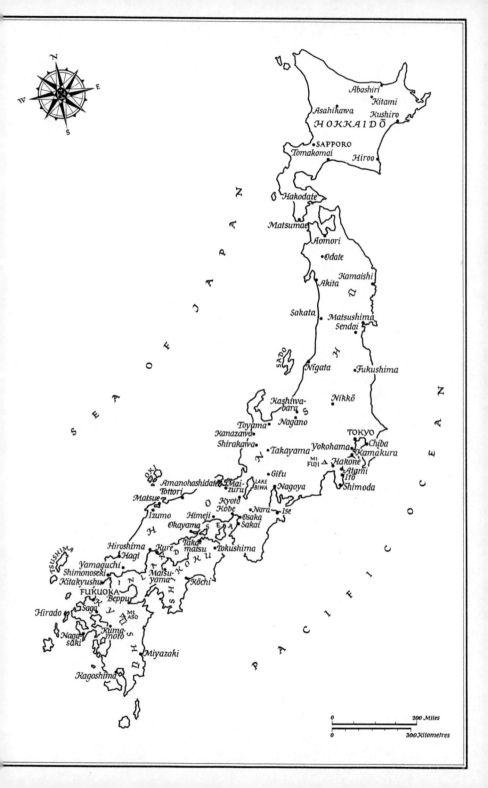

The *Bakufu* had received word of his arrival. Perry made it known that he would expect an answer in a year's time, when he would return in greater strength. This is what he did. The original request had caused great consternation, but the *Bakufu* realized that Japan was in no position to return a negative reply. Not merely did the Americans possess armaments greatly superior to those of the Japanese, but Japan, and not least Edo, was very vulnerable to attack. For one thing, Edo was supplied by Osaka by sea; and during the period of Perry's first stay, which was of ten days' duration, the service had to be suspended. The *daimyo* were consulted, and so was the Imperial Court. This latter move was especially significant, because sentiment in favour of the Emperor was still strong, and some *daimyo* had even begun to act as if, in respect of loyalty, the Emperor came before the Shogun. Reverence for the Emperor went by the name of *sōnnō*, and this was to play a part of increasing importance during the next few years. With *sōnnō* was combined another rallying-cry, *jōi*, so that together *sōnnō-jōi* signified: 'Revere the Emperor, expel the Barbarians.'

Many *daimyo* were against doing business with the foreigners. Consequently, when the *Bakufu* signed a treaty with Commodore Perry, which opened up the ports of Shimoda and Hakodate (in Hokkaido) to the Americans, there was much feeling against the Shogun. When a consular representative, Townsend Harris, installed himself in Shimoda, he was first ill received. But finally the Shogun consented to grant him an interview. No doubt the *Bakufu* were influenced by their knowledge that a British force had attacked and burnt Canton on account of the non-observance of a treaty. This humiliation of China gave the Japanese food for thought. Soon agreements were reached with Britain, Holland, Russia and France. These granted the foreigners substantial privileges, including extra-territorial rights. Forces hostile to the Tokugawas were incensed, and even the Imperial Court was against the treaties, at least to begin with. The hostility began to be directed more against the Shogun than against the foreign 'barbarians'. In 1859, diplomatic representatives of the powers arrived in Edo and took up permanent residence, and Yokohama became another port to admit foreign vessels. There was renewed hostility, and attacks on some foreigners were made, often by *rōnin*. Finally, alarmed at the trouble he had started, the Shogun, in a Canossa-like gesture for which there was no parallel in the relation between the military and Imperial government, took the road to Kyoto to consult the Emperor in person.

The Court ordered the *Bakufu* to expel the foreigners; but the Shogun, though he had apparently resolved to do this a little earlier, argued that such a move was now out of the question, and the Court reluctantly acquiesced. More trouble ensued. One incident in particular caused a great furore. An Englishman, Charles Richardson, riding along the highway near Yokohama, was thought by some retainers of the Satsuma clan, the clan occupying southern Kyushu, to have obstructed the passage of their *daimyo*, so they cut him down. The British government reacted strongly, and as all redress was refused, the British fleet bombarded Kagoshima. Traces of this bombardment can still be seen. This 'Namamugi Incident', as it was called, led to an interesting result.

This, and a number of other events, including peasant uprisings, brought the *Bakufu* into increasing unpopularity. And attempts to placate restive *daimyo*, such as the relaxation of the 'alternate attendance', had often the reverse effect: for the lords lost interest in the political life of Edo and began to consider their own interests exclusively. Another incident involving foreigners was when in 1863 the Chōshū clan fired on an American warship. This brought a reply from a combined flotilla of American, British, French and Dutch ships. In the case of Chōshū, as in the case of Satsuma, the result was unexpected: both clans, coming to terms with their enemies, cultivated something like friendship.

The *Bakufu* then got into worse difficulties. Some men from Chōshū tried to start a revolt in favour of the Emperor, the young man posthumously to be known as Meiji. Although the *Bakufu* troops succeeded in putting down the rebellion, with the help of Satsuma, they committed the error of trying to punish Chōshū more severely, by seeking to break up the clan altogether. At this, Satsuma rallied to the side of Chōshū, signing a treaty of friendship in 1866; and the *Bakufu* forces, though preponderant, were defeated. Perhaps it was as well for the *Bakufu* that at that moment the Shogun Iemochi died, and a truce was arranged.

The new Shogun, Keiki, decided upon reforms. In his desperation, he turned for help to the French minister in Edo. He had suspicions of the British, who were increasingly drawn towards the representatives of Chōshū and Satsuma and of all those opposed to the *Bakufu*.

Discontent among the *daimyo* soon led to Keiki's resignation, for it had been suggested that a Council of *daimyo* should be set up under Court patronage, and this was more than the Shogun was prepared to tolerate. Meanwhile, both Chōshū and Satsuma had managed to obtain the Emperor's support for action against the Tokugawa. The resulting *coup d'état* was led by Saigō Takamori, who was to play a tragic part in his later dealings with the Emperor. On 3 January 1868, the palace was taken, a council was summoned, Keiki was formally deprived of both office and lands, and, more important, responsibility for administering the country was vested in the Emperor. Strictly speaking, this last measure is better described as the return of power rather than as the conferring of it; and thus the event is known as the Meiji Restoration.

The *coup d'état* was not so brief an episode as has sometimes been suggested. Although Keiki had been nominally stripped of power, he was still not without supporters. Some of these even moved from Osaka, where Keiki had installed himself, to Kyoto. When they were repulsed, Keiki took refuge in Edo. At this, the Imperial forces began to march eastwards; and Keiki, seeing that resistance was useless, surrendered, though some Tokugawa supporters went on fighting for months, even in remote Hokkaido. In the end, Keiki was treated with great generosity. He was obliged to go into private life, but his successor as head of the Tokugawa clan was left territory almost equal to that controlled by Satsuma, and a good deal more than Chōshū. This accommodating settlement prevented bitterness and rivalry which might have done great damage to the new regime. There were many who assumed that a new Shogun, drawn from a different line, perhaps Satsuma or Chōshū, would be appointed; but soon it became clear that authority were better left in the hands of the Emperor. This was due partly to the Emperor's own character, for he showed himself to be a man of considerable ability. Indeed, today he is revered as a god.

It is only in retrospect that the Meiji Restoration appears to be the great and decisive event that it was. Some historians equate it with a great uprush of national feeling, and tend to infuse the whole event with an aura of myth. In fact, there was much 'touch and go' about it. Given the number of clans and personalities involved, things might so well have turned out differently. Some of Japan's great reformers, such as Fukuzawa Yūkichi (1835-1901), were by no means at first convinced of the rightness of the Emperor's cause. Fukuzawa was well ahead of his time in his ideas on education, and he had visited America in 1860; but his conversion to the Restoration was late, and in his remarkable *Autobiography* he freely admits the fact. Nor were the Tokugawa civil servants, some of them men of great ability, dismissed as were some of the higher functionaries. As smooth a transition as possible was made to the New Order.

For New Order there was. Few countries have ever formulated so explicitly a fresh national policy as Japan did at that time. The Atatürk Reform in Turkey, though remarkable, followed decades of foreign interference and even semi-occupation (capitulations, etc.); whereas Japan had put up the shutters in every window, so to speak, save in the Nagasaki enclave. The desire to remain apart must not be attributed to blind chauvinism. A Western thinker who was to become very popular in Meiji Japan, Herbert Spencer, on being asked for his opinion, recommended that Japan should as far as possible maintain her isolation. 'The Japanese policy should, I think, be', he wrote in 1892 to Baron Kentarō, 'that of *keeping Americans and Europeans as much as possible at arm's length*. In the presence of the more powerful races your position is one of chronic danger, and you should take every precaution to give as little foothold as possible to foreigners.'[1] He asked that this opinion should be kept in confidence, 'for I do not desire to rouse the animosity of my fellow-countrymen.' Yet the Meiji ministers, impressed by what they had seen of Western technology and by what they had learnt of Western science, made a definite *commitment* to modernization, and particularly to rapid industrialization. And, as if a head of steam had been built up during the Tokugawa period, the result was a mobilization of social energy, a communal advance, a breakthrough into the modern world.

Many observers, among them Lafcadio Hearn himself, regretted the innovations, while Basil Hall Chamberlain declared that the Old Japan was 'dead and gone'. Hearn was something of a sentimentalist, while Chamberlain, acute observer though he might be, could on occasion overstate his case. Innovation is something for which the Japanese have possessed a talent since the days of the China cultural missions. Conservation of the past, despite reform, is something without which they would cease to be the unique people they are.

1 The Inner Shrine of Ise, dedicated to the sun goddess Amaterasu Ōmikami. The shrines of Ise, ancient in foundation though periodically rebuilt in identical style, are constructed of cypress wood in the archaic Japanese manner.

2 Hanging scroll, or kakemono, by Sesshū (1420–1506), Zen priest and one of Japan's greatest painters. Almost abstract in its use of blank space and 'splashed-ink' shapes, it is typical of the Zen emphasis on intuition.

3 The bear-killing ceremony of the ancient Ainu. This ritual was preceded by apologies to the bear, who was treated as a god or *kamui*, and followed by feasting and dancing.

5 Seen from the air, one of the enormous burial mounds of the Tomb culture (about AD 350) clearly shows the characteristic 'keyhole' shape.

4 Pottery vessel of the middle Jōmon period (3rd millennium BC), made by people who had not the potter's wheel. It was found in Kamiina county, Nagano.

6 The five-storied pagoda of the Hōryūji temple at Nara, founded in 607 by Prince Umayado (574–622), posthumously known as Shōtoku Taishi.

7 Shōtoku Taishi, one of the first and most influential supporters of Buddhism in Japan, is shown here with his two children.

8 *Left* The Daibutsu, o
Great Buddha, in the
Tōdaiji temple at Nar
one of the oldest
religious monuments
in Japan.

9 *Below:* Statues of
Kannon, the Goddess
of Mercy, in the San-
jūsangendō or Renge-
o-in temple at Kyoto.

10, 11 Two men of outstanding ability who achieved the reunification of Japan in the sixteenth century: Nobunaga (*left*) and his successor and one-time vassal, Hideyoshi.

12 Francis Xavier, Jesuit and missionary, made many converts in his two years in Japan. He called the Japanese 'the delight of his heart'.

13 Night scene in the Yoshi wara quarter of Edo – the entertainment and 'red-ligh district of what is now Tokyo.

14 First contact with the West: a Japanese impression of the Portuguese merchant who came to Japan in the 1540's.

15, 16 The two greatest masters of that purely Japanese art, the wood-block print or *ukiyo-e* (pictures of 'the floating world'), are Hokusai and Hiroshige. *Above:* One of Hokusai's famous 'Thirty-six views of Mount Fuji'. *Below:* No. 53 in the set of 'Fifty-three posting stations on the Tōkaidō Road', by Hiroshige.

17 Procession of one of the powerful feudal lords, or *daimyo*. When he passed, escorted by his armed retainers, the common people found it safest to prostrate themselves.

7   From medieval to modern

ALTHOUGH IT MUST NOT be supposed that the Meiji policy of reform met with no opposition, there were men who, impressed by what had already been achieved, advocated reforms bordering on the wildly impractical. One minister of education, who was assassinated for his temerity, advocated the substitution of English for Japanese as the national language. A writer went so far as to suggest, though without suffering the same fate, that Japanese men should take European wives in order to improve the stature and virility of the race. In short, Westernization became a craze, just as it had done when the Portuguese had arrived centuries earlier. The top hat and morning coat became the new uniform, and so they have remained. Paris fashions were scrupulously followed. As Basil Hall Chamberlain said: 'To have lived through the transition stage of modern Japan makes a man feel preternaturally old; for here he is in modern times . . . and yet he himself can distinctly remember the Middle Ages.'[1]

The mechanics of government during the transition period became a preoccupation of the 'new men', as an entirely new system had to be created. The country was divided up into administrative districts, and a consultative assembly was summoned. In April 1868, a statement of policy was issued in the name of the Emperor: it was called the Charter Oath. This made it clear that though 'base customs of former times shall be abolished', the people's wishes should be consulted on all broad questions of policy. Later on, an Executive Council was set up, to which a number of samurai were appointed as advisers. These mostly came from Satsuma and Chōshū, together with Tosa and Hizen, domains in the west. As these men came to prominence, the Consultative Council fell into abeyance, for its purpose had been largely to demonstrate upon how much support the new regime could count. Thus a new and powerful oligarchy came into being. Composed of men of similar background and outlook, it dominated public life for the next forty years.

To break up the feudal structure of society was not easy, but every effort was made to do so. Samurai who held public office were obliged to sever all connection with their former domains. The Tokugawa lands, instead of being distributed as rewards to *daimyo*, were put under Imperial patronage.[2] As a gesture of loyalty, the four principal domains 'surrendered' their property to the Emperor, and obliged other *daimyo* to follow suit. What this boiled down to was that the *daimyo*, while retaining authority in their former domains, became imperial officials. Domains were formally abolished in 1871, and renamed prefectures (*Ken*). Local military forces were disbanded, and the army became a centralized force under the government. A new taxation system was introduced, so that the government became for the first time solvent. Meanwhile, the seat of government had been transferred to Edo, the name of which was changed to Tokyo, and the Emperor moved from his Kyoto palace to the Shogun's castle.

Much influenced by Western traditions, especially those of England, the entire order of 'society' was transformed. The Court nobility and the feudal lords became the peerage, which from 1884 was split into five ranks. The old retainers became the gentry. There was temporarily a rank for lesser feudal dignitaries. Those without titles or privileges, namely the bulk of the population, were labelled commoners. Thus the old caste division of samurai, peasant, artisan and merchant vanished, though the social influence of these divisions, especially that of samurai, remained.

More radical a measure, the old divisions between Imperial Court and Shogunal *Bakufu* disappeared, thus altering a governmental structure which had endured for centuries and to which the Emperor system probably owed its survival. The abolition of the classes entailed permission to intermarry, so that commoners could form alliances with members of the peerage. This measure had important consequences.

All such changes made for national unity. With the introduction of conscription in 1872, the samurai lost their military monopoly, and all that remained for them was prestige. In 1871, a Ministry of Education was established, and a compulsory system of primary education planned. Since Great Britain had introduced a similar measure only the year before, Japan's rapid progress from a medieval to a modern state may be appreciated. Under a Department of Public Works set up in 1870, an extensive telegraph system was introduced, and with British advice a railway was constructed from Tokyo to Osaka and Kobe. Much of this work was undertaken in record time, and amid great public enthusiasm.

Growing confidence made some Japanese statesmen uneasy at the treaties which the Tokugawas had been obliged to sign with the Western powers. It was therefore decided to send a mission to Europe in order to seek their revision. Headed by the leading statesmen Ōkubo, Kido and Itō, the mission stayed away for eighteen months. Washington, Berlin and London were visited. But the mission did not prove successful. The Western Governments insisted that more reforms would have to be carried out, especially in Japan's legal system, before a discussion of treaty revision could be entertained.

The mission returned to Japan in full awareness that such reform measures were incumbent. As it happened, they found a situation of unexpected gravity. Japan's relations with Korea had taken a turn for the worse when that country had refused Japan's demand to establish relations. To Japan's annoyance, Korea had insisted upon remaining in seclusion, whereas many Japanese statesmen saw in that country a useful outlet for Japanese expansion, together with a chance for the samurai, who had lost so much by the reforms, to regain some material advantage. One of the most enthusiastic advocates of this aggressive policy was the picturesque character from Satsuma, Saigō Takamori. The returning statesmen opposed him on the grounds that reform at home was more urgent than war abroad. A bitter quarrel broke out; and for the first time the ruling oligarchy, to which Saigō belonged, was split in its counsels. Saigō and others resigned. An opposition came into being. While this rift was no doubt good for Japanese democratic development, it brought early tragedy with it.

Some members of the opposition provoked revolts, and one of the insurgents was Saigō himself. He mobilized the samurai of his part of Kyushu (Satsuma), where he had remained very much the feudal lord. Although a warrior and a man of action, he was a passionate believer in education, and he had set up many schools, mostly for samurai. He had also invited to Kagoshima, the provincial capital,

Dr William Willis, an Irish doctor, who set up a hospital there, which later became the Faculty of Medicine of the University.

Urged on by his followers, Saigō set out to march on the capital. It was a daring escapade, and it met with its first check in Kyushu itself, for the government garrison at Kumamoto put up such a fierce resistance that Saigō was pinned down for months in the southernmost island. But he was a man of extreme stubbornness, and, when attacked, he held out against 40,000 men for six months before being driven back to Kagoshima. Here in September 1877, with all hope of victory gone, he retired to a cave and committed hara-kiri. Like the story of the forty-seven *rōnin*, Saigō's rebellion seems to have touched a chord in the Japanese psyche, for his memory still arouses passionate devotion, not least in Kagoshima, where the place of his death is shown with reverence. Perhaps there is another reason for the Saigō cult. His rebellion was the last of a long series of feudal uprisings, and it has therefore acquired something of a romantic aura. Romantic it was: for never again were the samurai to go into battle wielding their precious swords. Not that their influence disappeared. Many of them continued to be restive under the new regime, and they were largely responsible for another feature of Japanese political life, namely assassination.

The formation of an opposition led to the establishment of parties. A liberal party was formed by Itagaki and Gotō, and a progressive party by Ōkuma. These moves required some courage, as the government had taken strong measures to suppress hostile opinion. Nevertheless, it was from about 1888 that the first great newspapers began to exert influence by critical editorials. One of these organs was the *Mainichi*, still among the most powerful of Japanese journals; another was the *Yūbin Hōchi*, controlled by Ōkuma. Above all, they provided a forum of debate, despite strict government control, about the measure which everyone was now discussing, namely a Constitution designed to provide for a National Assembly. Much attention was paid to the various provisions of this Constitution. In 1882 Itō spent eighteen months abroad studying the institutions of other countries. He visited Berlin and Vienna, and he later went to France and to England where he conferred with Herbert Spencer. The Constitution itself was promulgated in 1889, after discussions which were for the most part private. It affirmed the supreme authority of the Emperor, and provided for a European-style parliamentary and cabinet system, though the cabinet was not responsible to the two chambers. The prime minister was to be chosen by a group of elder statesmen, or *genrō*.

The Constitution was decidedly authoritarian, for the Emperor had powers of constitutional revision, of declaring war, concluding treaties, and adjourning or proroguing the assembly (or the Diet, as it was called), even though he would act only upon advice. The House of Peers was vested with powers equal to those of the Lower House; and as the former was packed with supporters of the regime, the influence of the latter was severely circumscribed.

Out of a population of about 40 million, a bare 500,000 citizens were qualified to vote, and the parliamentary deliberations in 1890 got off to a somewhat shaky start. The elections of 1892 were less than orderly; a bitter electoral campaign left 25 dead and about 400 injured. The Diet was in a hostile mood, and another election in 1892 ended with the dissolution of the Lower House after a month. These were the inevitable growing pains of a new democracy.

Meanwhile, special measures had been taken in the sphere of education. In 1882, the government had introduced courses in elementary schools on moral teaching, which included some strict views on sexual ethics; and in an important Rescript on Education, promulgated in 1890, reverence for the Emperor was encouraged, together with the adoption of the virtues of filial piety, respect for authority, and loyalty to the group. This demonstrated that Confucianism was by no means dead. Indeed, there was an official at Court whose task it was to teach it. School attendance had reached a high level. By 1880, the compulsory period of education was three years, being raised to four in 1886. Attendance had reached 60 per cent by 1895, 90 per cent by 1900, and 95 per cent by 1906. Thus Japan had achieved a standard of basic education which no other Asian country could emulate, or has since approached. In 1886, Tokyo Imperial University was established, the result of merging together a number of institutions of higher learning.

About this time there grew up renewed interest in Christianity, the ban on which had been lifted in 1873; but although this revival gave rise to the resumption of foreign missionary activity, and also to the emergence of the pathetic Christian 'underground', certain Japanese, notably Uchimura Kanzō (1861-1930), felt that the Christian Church, or rather Western ecclesiastical organization, was ill adapted to Japanese society. They therefore started what was called the 'non-church movement'. It was through this movement above all that Christian ideas permeated many levels of Japanese society, so that Christian influence remained out of all proportion to the number of formal adherents.

Without a durable social structure, especially at the level of the peasantry, the educational progress of Japan would hardly have been possible. In the early days, village life had been closely integrated, with villages joining together in groups or 'federations', supervised by a headman who acquired great power and respect. Then there was the 'ten-man group' (*jūnin-gumi*) of peasants, introduced by Hideyoshi and paralleled by the 'five-man group' (*gonin-gumi*) of samurai, which exercised collective responsibility for local affairs. Instead of the family, in the restricted Western sense, the unit was the collective household or *ie*, and it was no doubt part of their genius for assimilation that led the Japanese to cultivate *adoption* as a means of perpetuating the household unit. Although there were exceptions to the rule, the importance which the head of the family attached to securing a suitable son-in-law might impel him to adopt a daughter in order that by her marriage he might obtain the desired successor. At all costs, the little community must be ensured continuance; and in order to make this possible, the household, to cite an academic but accurate definition, was 'conceptualized in the time-continuum from past to future, including not only the actual residential members but also dead members, with some projection also towards those yet unborn.'[3] This explained in part the respect accorded to age; for in agricultural districts above all, the household was an 'enterprise with insurance for old members'.[4] It was also the custom for the head of the family and his wife to move, at the moment when age dictated, to a smaller residence in the household compound, where they could continue to live their own life while remaining in close touch with the rest of the family. This was called the *Inkyo* system. Finally, the family contained members or underlings (*genin*) who were not blood relations at all. Even as late as 1920, 74 per cent of families were of this traditional *ie* type.

During the Meiji period, great efforts were made to encourage agricultural production by adopting Western methods. For this purpose, missions were sent to Europe and America, and foreign experts were invited to Japan. It was an era of experimentation. A campaign for developing more land was initiated, and the northern-most island, Hokkaido, hitherto barely explored, received intensive cultivation.⁵ In Sapporo, one of the most important agricultural colleges was founded, under the direction of an American, Dr William S. Clark, whose reputation is revered to this day. The college eventually became Hokkaido University. Since rice was the sacred food, it was planted intensively in Hokkaido, though the soil and climate were far from suited to it. Attempts in other regions to grow the vine and to introduce sheep-farming proved less successful.

Between 1880 and 1894, rice production increased by more than 30 per cent, and yields equally impressive characterized the production of wheat and barley. At the same time, fisheries were encouraged, and Japan soon had the most flourishing fishing industry in Asia. Cotton production rose, though later competition from India caused a marked decline. Above all, the silk industry flourished, and raw silk came to form about a third of the national export trade.

As the greater part of the population was still agricultural, the tax-revenue it yielded remained a major source of government funds. Moreover, agricultural exports served to pay for much of the machinery and raw materials needed for industry. And it was heavy industry above all that the Meiji politicians wished to develop.

The spectacular material transformation of the country proved a source of pride to the ordinary Japanese. With determination and will-power, it seemed that almost anything on the material plane could be accomplished. Interest was focused upon the 'secret' of Western success, and translations of books such as Samuel Smiles's *Self-Help* became best-sellers (1870). In this movement of enlightenment, Fukuzawa Yūkichi was a leading figure. The curiosity regarding things Western extended to the subject of manners both public and private: for now that the classes were abolished, no one knew exactly how to behave with propriety. One *daimyo* enquired how he should treat dancing-girls: should they be summoned openly to public restaurants or secretly to private houses? His enquiry concluded: 'At this time of innovation, we should like to know the correct way to conduct ourselves.' On a more serious level, information and guidance were repeatedly sought on the problem of raising Japan to the level of the more powerful nations of the West. Even the early translation of *Robinson Crusoe* contained a preface pointing out that the book could provide information on how to develop an island.[6] Indeed, it was not untrue to say that 'a disciplined and largely humourless quest characterized the Meiji period.'[7]

Yet, with all the extravagances to which certain enthusiasts for Westernization were impelled, the traditional teachings were not forgotten. Nor were they necessarily out of harmony with some aspects of the Westernizing movement. The Confucian idea of a natural order was not incompatible with Western ideas of internationalism; and despite their chauvinistic tendencies, the modern Japanese have always clung to the idea of a world order, no doubt controlled or influenced by Japan, but nevertheless a system transcending national boundaries. This was part of their idealism, and it emerged at unexpected moments.

The preoccupation with treaty revision persisted, because it was felt that Japan had suffered unjustly at a time when she was too weak to help herself. Thus, coeval with the movement towards Westernization was an intense patriotic upsurge, together with a feeling that Japan, with her new national image, should rightfully assume leadership in Asia, above all in the role of liberator from Western exploitation. There was also the growing conviction that Japan, a small but energetic country, needed an 'outlet' on the continent. Now the two countries most likely to provide such an outlet were Korea and China, but the matter was complicated by the fact that China regarded Korea as a vassal state. As a result, a quarrel broke out in 1884 in which Chinese and Japanese forces came to blows. There was another dispute a decade later; and as it was now a question of whether China or Japan should control Korea, and as Japan had taken over certain installations in Seoul, including the royal palace, China felt that she had no alternative but to fight for her rights.

She was over-confident. From the outset, Chinese troops were subjected to defeat after crushing defeat. Japan not merely took over the greater part of Korea, but she moved up into Manchuria (October 1894). A second Japanese army attacked Liaotung, captured Port Arthur, and, by February 1895, had occupied Weihaiwei. When it became clear that the Japanese were about to advance on Peking, China sued for peace. The resulting treaty ended all Chinese claims over Korea, and ceded Formosa (Taiwan) to Japan, as well as the Liaotung peninsula and Port Arthur. In addition, China was obliged to pay a substantial indemnity.

Japan had secured a victory far beyond her expectations. But this very achievement alarmed the other great powers. There were vigorous protests from Russia, France and Germany about the acquisition of the Liaotung peninsula. Japan was advised to hand this territory back to China. The motives behind the protest were mixed. The reason most frequently put forward was that a permanent Japanese foothold in China would seriously disturb the peace of the area. Exhausted by the war, and unwilling to incur the hostility of three major powers, Japan found herself in the humiliating position of having to submit, though in exchange for Liaotung she was to gain an increased indemnity. The effect at home was naturally to arouse widespread indignation. Despite her astonishing victory, Japan was being treated almost as one of the vanquished. She was being dictated to by Western powers. Nettled, she set about increasing her military strength. This was in order to counter another possible Triple Intervention, as the Western move had been called, and in order to strengthen her general position against nations which, observing China's weakness, were moving in to 'protect their interests'.

In China, a violent anti-foreign movement sprang up. It culminated in the Boxer Rebellion of 1900. The Boxers, members of a secret society,[8] occupied the approaches to Peking and attacked the foreign legations. There was an immediate reaction by the countries concerned; but as Japan was best placed to intervene, her troops were the first and most powerful contingent to move into the capital. This swift and well-conducted move served to enhance her reputation. The nation that chose to take no part in this action was Russia. Indeed, Russia behaved in a manner calculated to give great offence to Japan: for when the Boxer troubles provoked disturbances in north-west China, Russia used this as an excuse to occupy the whole of Manchuria. The result was a rapprochement between the two powers most anxious to prevent Russian expansion, namely Japan and Britain.

There was much else to bring them together, above all the fact that the two countries were collaborating over reform, and that as seafaring nations lying off a continent they enjoyed community of interests. Hence a far-reaching agreement signed in January 1902. As Japan had secured an understanding with the most powerful of Western nations, the agreement was hailed at home with enthusiasm.

Even today, the alliance with Britain is still remembered with a kind of nostalgia.

Following the alliance, Russia began withdrawing her forces from Manchuria, but she failed to complete the operation, and tension accordingly built up between her and Japan. Instead of being dissuaded by the Anglo-Japanese agreement, Russia became even more high-handed, making demands in respect of China and Manchuria which Japan found quite unacceptable. On 10 February 1902, the two countries found themselves at war. Although Russian troops entered Korea, Japan defeated the Russian fleet off Port Arthur and soon pushed the Russians back into Manchuria. Another army landed on the Liaotung peninsula. Port Arthur was laid under siege, and Mukden captured. Finally, most crushing of blows, the Russian fleet, which had made a long voyage from European waters, was totally destroyed by Admiral Tōgō in the Tsushima Straits.

With American mediation, peace negotiations were opened at Portsmouth, New Hampshire. Japan obtained less than she wanted, but even so it was substantial: predominance in Korea, rights in Manchuria and China, half of Sakhalin (Karafuto), and Liaotung. The real achievement, however, was the fact that she had gained a victory over a major European power. Within a short while of emerging from isolation, she had become the dominating power in Asia, confirmed in what she believed to be her 'imperial mission'. Her victory sent a tremor of anxiety through the Western world.

This time Japan was quick to exploit her victory. Her supremacy over Korea was soon recognized, and Itō, now a Prince, took up the position of Resident General. Nevertheless, Korean resistance was strong, and Itō was murdered in 1909. This was used as an excuse for total annexation. Japan also consolidated her position in Manchuria, where her predominant commercial interests were recognized. Although some Western powers, including Britain, were extremely worried, the Anglo-Japanese Alliance was renewed for the second time in 1911 (the first was in 1905).

The first sign that Japan, or rather that a group of militarist-minded statesmen, was bent upon systematic aggression abroad was to be observed when, during the First World War, she made her 'twenty-one demands' on China, which had become a Republic in 1912. These were so harsh as to alienate even Japan's allies. Meanwhile, Japan had declared war on Germany on 23 August 1914, and within a short while she had mopped up all Germany's interests in the Far East. China was obliged to give in to the 'demands', which had been slightly modified. At the Peace Conference, Japan, though having fought comparatively little, enjoyed the status of one of the victorious powers. Her position was further stabilized when Britain, America, France and Japan met in 1921 and agreed to respect each other's rights and gains. This Four-Power Agreement spelt the end of the Anglo-Japanese Alliance, which by 1923 had lapsed altogether. The Agreement was followed by a joint naval treaty which left Japan the chief sea power in the Western Pacific and in command of all the approaches to China. China's position was settled by a Nine-Power Treaty, which included the signatories of the Four-Power Pact. Although Chinese sovereignty was formally recognized, Japan's economic interests were recognized too, and Japan's Asiatic dominance was confirmed. Japan's great military success over the past decades had made her army a force in cabinet decisions. Indeed, the army had become a force in making decisions on its own without reference to the civil arm. This tendency was ominously to increase in the post-war period, until there came a point when the army could control the very existence of a cabinet by threatening, in the case of a measure to which it was opposed, the resignation of its nominee.

After the cessation of hostilities in 1918, Japan enjoyed an era of prosperous liberalism. Great economic growth was attained, and this was reflected in the power of commercial organizations or trading houses, known as *zaibatsu*. The most prominent of these were Mitsui, Mitsubishi, Yasuda and Sumitomo. They covered a wide range of economic enterprise: banking, heavy industry, shipping etc. These giants, which had grown up during the Meiji period, were founded by merchants (Mitsui) as well as by former samurai (Mitsubishi). Despite their size and enormous ramifications, they remained for the most part 'family affairs', consolidated by shrewd marriage-alliances and by useful connections in the political sphere. Hence they came to wield considerable political influence, and their contracts often favoured the military. They could also provide enormous entertainments, exhibiting conspicuous consumption which was itself socially influential. On the other hand, the *zaibatsu* served to offset the presence of numerous small firms, also family enterprises, and the fact that half the population still worked on the land.

There was thus a widening gap between rich and poor; and the growth of cities, even though on the whole small compared with the enormous conurbations of Tokyo–Yokohama and Osaka, created much overcrowding and squalor. Of the land area of Japan, only about 16 per cent proved habitable, and population was growing fast. Yet the people as a whole were a good deal better off than they had been before the war. A new middle class was in formation; and with the egalitarian educational system, this class began to acquire considerable political influence by sheer weight of numbers. Public taste matched itself to the economic status of the individual. Whereas the rich could afford geisha, and might even use them on occasion for confidential negotiations, the ordinary man patronized the tea-houses and bars which were springing up everywhere, sometimes constituting whole 'entertainment areas'. Here hostesses helped to relax the tensions of business men after a day at the office, and something called a 'bar life' grew up, which entered into the day-to-day experience. of the commoners. From this world the wife and mother was excluded. Her lot was far less varied and interesting.

While there was economic growth, there remained a measure of political instability. Cabinets were formed and dissolved, often as a result of an assassination. The normal form of government was that of coalition, with factions competing for places, and with the army in the background intriguing and wielding increasing influence. The real decisions or 'bargains' tended thus to be made outside the Diet altogether. Bribery was practised by individuals and by organizations. These conditions, together with discontent in town and country – for, despite prosperity, there were strikes on account of inflation and high taxation – gave rise to much left-wing agitation. In the early years of the century, there had been unsuccessful attempts to found a Socialist party, while a Communist party, though short-lived, was set up in 1921. Unions had been founded in the 1890's, and after the war their power increased, with a breakaway communist-dominated movement in 1925. Both the left-wing parties and the unions were harassed by police action; for in 1925, a law was passed making it illegal to agitate to overthrow the governmental system or to abolish private ownership. Such a measure could be directed against left-wing opinion in general, and many who were not extremists suffered from its application. Even torture, officially abolished under the Meiji Constitution, was in some cases employed. Such pressure had the effect of uniting the radical movement, hitherto split by faction, in the Social Mass Party (*Shakai Taishūtō*) in 1932, and this obtained some power in the Diet.

Nevertheless, a great weight of public opinion still drew its inspiration from the old traditions of Japan, and in particular from the idea that Japan, whatever it may have learnt from the West, was the appointed leader in Asia against Western domination. Emperor-worship still encouraged the belief that the Japanese were a unique people, descended from the gods, and destined ultimately to rule the world. Many patriotic societies flourished, and some that were secret, with a belligerent ideology. One of the most powerful of these latter was the Society for the Preservation of the National Essence (*Yūzon-sha*), founded by a violent fanatic, Kita Ikki, who was also a writer. His book *An Outline Plan for the Reconstruction of Japan* was, though officially forbidden, enormously popular. Apart from radical domestic measures, it advocated a policy of imperial expansion. For its radicalism did not prevent its preaching loyalty to the Emperor. This loyalty was common to other radical manifestoes. All these movements depended upon violence for the realization of their aims. That they should have attracted many elements in the armed services was not surprising. A right-wing nationalist radicalism emerged, with an anti-capitalist (and therefore anti-*zaibatsu*) bias, and a hostility to the political parties. It arrogated to itself the monopoly of patriotism, and anyone who stood out against its principles was branded as disloyal.

This movement acquired greater power as a result of the world slump of 1929–30, which was brought about by the great American recession. There was a disastrous fall in Japan's cotton exports, and in raw silk prices. Nationalists were also enraged by the London Naval Treaty of 1930, which limited Japan's fleet to a point below that which was considered essential for the proposed expansion of sea-power.

Finally, plots began to be hatched. Two in 1931 proved abortive, but they were followed by an 'incident' in Manchuria, probably deliberately provoked, as a result of which the so-called Kwantung Army proceeded to occupy Mukden and then a larger area of the country. This move was backed by the government at home, though on first hearing rumours of it, efforts had been made to restrain the army. Unfortunately, the war minister and the General Staff were wholeheartedly in favour of military action, and they encouraged the

93

spread of hostilities to China. Soon the whole of Manchuria was once again under Japanese domination, and this time there was no looking back. Declaring that Manchuria was now independent of China, Japan set up in March 1932 a puppet state called Manchukuo, with the Manchu emperor, Pu Yi, the last of his line, as its puppet monarch.

At home, the nationalists were overjoyed. Ministers known to disapprove of their policy were attacked, and in May 1932, after a *putsch*, the prime minister was assassinated. Although trials followed, the sentences imposed were light. An attempt was made to reassert parliamentary control, but it was largely ineffective. Meanwhile, two groups within the army engaged in a struggle for power: the Imperial Way faction (*Kōdō*) and the Control faction (*Tōsei*), the first regarding Russia as Japan's chief rival, and the second advocating even stronger measures in Manchuria and China. In 1936 the *Kōdō* group staged a *coup d'état* by occupying buildings in the centre of Tokyo and attacking the prime minister's house. As a result of mistaken identity, the premier, Okada, escaped, though the highly respected finance minister, Takahashi, and others were brutally murdered. The followers of *Kōdō* evidently assumed that by their action they would precipitate a popular uprising, but in this they were mistaken. The Emperor ordered the Navy and the Imperial Guards to throw a ring round the rebels. Balloons with suspended messages were sent up calling for their surrender. A few days later the *Kōdō* gave in. There were swift executions, and a little later their ideologist Kita Ikki himself was executed.

By the suppression of this uprising, discipline was temporarily restored in the army, and many of the progressives took heart. Henceforward it was agreed, by the resurrection of a former ruling, that the war minister must be an acting serving officer, thereby keeping him from excessive political intervention. Radical young officers were sent abroad or to distant provinces. But the military agitation continued in another guise. This was sometimes known as *gekokujō*, which means approximately that superiors are at the dictates of inferiors; this gave increasing power to officers, who manipulated the decision-making politicians.[9] The government therefore came under the control of the services: a system which began to operate successfully under the influence of the *Tōsei* faction, which was now uppermost.

94

Since the services could claim to have obeyed the Emperor's command to save the nation, nothing could stop the movement towards military control, which, beginning as an aspiration, had now become a reality. The next few years saw the service chiefs virtually choosing the prime minister. Even when the respected Prince Konoe was brought in as a supposedly suitable nominee, his life was made uncomfortable and finally impossible because of the army. The civil government and its well-wishers, of which there were many, had been placed in a dilemma. They had suppressed the *Kōdō* faction, only to suffer the *Tōsei* in its place. And the latter, because of its imperialist leanings, was proving in many ways more intractable than the former.

8   Co-Prosperity and war

THE RESULT WAS that Japan drifted into war almost like a somnambulist. In July 1937, there was another 'incident', this time at the Marco Polo bridge not far from Peking. Precisely how this skirmish occurred between Japanese and Chinese troops is not known, but there is reason to believe that it was a deliberately provoked conspiracy by the Japanese. Soon the fighting extended, but the Japanese were surprised to find that Chinese resistance was exceptionally tough. As usual, the government at home was nervous. So indeed were some members of the army, but for purely military reasons: they realized that if their forces became embroiled too deeply in China, the chances of Russian aggression in an exposed Manchuria were the greater. In the end, however, the army extremists had their way. Support from home was promised. Peking and Tientsin were occupied; there was a flare-up of fighting in Shanghai; and soon, by a move up the Yangtse, Nanking, the capital, was taken. Here, the reputation of the Japanese as clean and honourable fighters, adhering to the samurai code, was badly smirched. To this day, despite what was to come, the appalling behaviour of the troops is remembered with bitterness and horror. Chiang Kai-shek moved his capital to Chungking, appealing to the League of Nations, which Japan had left in 1933 at the time of her 'recognition' of Manchukuo; but no help was forthcoming from that quarter, and Japan resolved to pursue her advantage. Towards the end of 1938, she had occupied the major part of China. Prince Konoe then announced plans for a New Order in Asia. The first stage in the establishment of Japanese Asiatic leadership had been achieved.

Having come so far, Japan found it necessary to consolidate her gains. Just as she had established a puppet regime in Manchukuo, so she attempted the same thing in Nanking, where in March 1940 she installed Wang Ching-wei, who had deserted Chiang Kai-shek's Kuomintang, as head of the government. Nevertheless, Japan did not find pacification easy. Both Chiang Kai-shek and the Chinese Communists organized a guerrilla resistance, which, like the Chinese resistance in general, the Japanese found surprisingly strong and resilient. Hence Japan never managed to conquer China. And the later announcement of a Greater East Asia Co-Prosperity Sphere had little more than verbal significance, though by that time other conquests had seemed to justify it.

Meanwhile, the country had been moving towards a still more dangerous imbroglio. Japan's fears of Russia, which seemed justified in view of several sharp incidents on the Manchurian, Siberian and Mongolian border, made her turn to the ally whose policy was no less anti-Communist than her own. This was Hitler's Germany. The Anti-Comintern Pact had been signed in November 1936, and discussions thereafter proceeded for even closer collaboration. Since the outbreak of war in September 1939, the Japanese military had been certain of Germany's victory. For that reason, they pushed for a more open alliance, which culminated in the signing of the Tripartite Pact between Japan, Germany and Italy in September 1940. In order further to alleviate her fears of Russia, Japan signed a neutrality agreement with the Soviet Union in April 1941. Meanwhile, a peripatetic diplomat, Matsuoka Yōsuke, had been visiting the world's capitals, putting Japan's 'case'. He was in fact prospecting the new international set-up following upon the supposedly imminent Axis victory. Two events upset his, and many another diplomat's, calculations. The first was the continued resistance of Britain; the second was the attack, in June 1941, by Germany upon the Soviet Union. Of this attack Japan had received no warning.

Although he was dropped as foreign minister in a July cabinet reshuffle, Matsuoka had achieved a good deal during his term of office. He had worked out details for Japan's expansion in South-East Asia: an expansion which he and his imperialist-minded friends considered to be essential for Japan's future. The plan was nothing less than to occupy Indo-China, Siam, Burma, Malaya and the Dutch East Indies. After that, there was the possibility, and as the Axis advanced the probability, of linking up with German forces, perhaps in India, as Hitler was determined to thrust through to Iraq and Iran in order to capture their much-needed oil. Japan's expansion in Asia would give her the raw materials of which she stood in need, particularly oil, tin and rubber. A start had been made when Vichy France, virtually helpless, agreed in September 1940 to allow Japan to establish air bases in Indo-China, and to permit the passage of troops. In return, Japan recognized, for what it was worth, France's sovereignty over the country. She then put pressure on the Dutch East Indies, hoping to obtain oil from that quarter, but here her diplomacy met with a check. What Japan hoped to avoid, at least as long as she could, was a confrontation with the United States, and the story of her negotiations with that country is a long, complicated, and controversial one. Assuming that she did not become involved with America, she had two alternatives: to go north and attack a Soviet Union at grips with the Nazi invader, or to go south, as was her immediate preference, trusting that such a move would not drive America into open war. As it was, America had reacted sharply to Japanese moves in China and Indo-China; and by July 1941, when Japan had all but occupied Indo-China, trade relations between the two countries had, at America's insistence, virtually been terminated.

The burden of Japan's negotiations with the United States was that Japan should obtain the rubber and oil she needed and secure her position in China, whereas America was insisting precisely that Japan should relinquish her ambitions in China and South-East Asia. From the beginning, the differences appeared irreconcilable; but although it was clear that neither side wanted war, both sides realized that war might come, and there was in Japan a party, namely the *Tōsei*, which, believing in Japan's mission and invincibility, was prepared to welcome it. On the other hand, the feeling for peace among large sections of the population must not be underestimated. Writing in 1936, an acute Japanese observer, Nohara Komakichi, observed: 'The Pacific Ocean will remain the Pacific Ocean: we should not disturb its repose . . . whoever resorted to arms today would commit a grave crime for which atonement could never be made.'[1] And the Social Mass Party, with its large membership, was resolutely against the militarists, so much so that the American ambassador, Joseph C. Grew, whose record of painstaking negotiation and shrewd under- standing has sometimes been impugned, wrote in his diary for 1 January 1937: 'Protest from the people is the significant new factor in Japanese politics. As the year 1937 opens, popular opposition to the government's policies is making itself felt with greater emphasis than at any time since before 1931. Cabinets in the past have been subject to opposition pressure, but for many years no opposition has so directly derived from the people themselves.'[2]

We now know that the Japanese staff had made the most detailed plans should war become necessary. It was agreed that hostilities should start at the latest by December 1941. Prince Konoe had worked hard for peace, but when he felt that his efforts were getting nowhere, he resigned. That was on 16 October 1941. He was succeeded by General Tōjō Hideki, of the War Ministry. No doubt the civilians hoped that such a man would be able to exert control over the services, but the reverse happened. The wishes of the militants became dominant.

Once Japan had decided to strike south, the main preoccupation of the war-planners was summed up in one problem, namely how to eliminate the American Pacific fleet; for this was the great threat to Japanese expansionist moves. The main base for that fleet was Pearl Harbor in Honolulu. Here, on 7 December 1941, a Sunday, Japanese planes, operating from ships which, ten days before, had left the Kurile Islands to the north of Japan, carried out a bombing and torpedoing raid which in a brief period knocked out the greater part of America's sea and air strength. Complete surprise was achieved. Yet, ironically enough, the possibility of an attack had been entertained and reported, especially by Joseph Grew. As early as 27 December 1934, Grew recorded in his diary that the Netherlands Minister in Tokyo, General Pabst, had told him that the Japanese navy, wishing to emulate the army, 'would be perfectly capable of descending upon and occupying Guam at a moment of crisis, or, indeed, at any other moment, regardless of the ulterior consequences.' Grew also records, on 25 April 1936, Pabst's view that 'there was a 50/50 chance that the Japanese navy would attempt a *coup de main* within six months, with the objective of taking possession of New Guinea or Borneo or some part of the Netherlands Indies producing petroleum.' Again, on 1 October 1940, Grew reflected that, if the United States tried to prevent Japanese expansion, 'retaliation might assume the shape of measures by the Government to counter our export embargos, but there would be a still greater probability of some sudden move by the army or navy taken unbeknown to the Government or without its prior authorization'. But Grew's most significant remark was that recorded on 27 January 1941, namely, that 'there is a lot of talk around town to the effect that the Japanese, in case of a break with the United States, are planning to go all out in a surprise attack on Pearl Harbor. Of course I informed our Government.'[3]

It is difficult to know why these and other warnings were not heeded, especially as the Americans had finally broken the Japanese code. According to some authorities, Grew was considered by the State Department to be 'old-fashioned and honourable but gullible'.[4]

Despite the breaking of the code, the Americans had failed to establish strict security at Pearl Harbor. From the small Japanese consulate in Honolulu, a young man of twenty-nine, Yoshikawa Takio, re-named Morimura Tadashi, engaged in bold espionage operations. He was often accompanied in his 'tours' of the islands by an attractive geisha, counting and identifying battleships, and even diving one night into Pearl Harbor itself in order to ascertain whether an anti-submarine net was in place.[5] It was not. There was also another man operating in New Mexico, overtly an assistant naval attaché, Commander Wachi Tsunezō, but in fact chief of Japan's overseas espionage ring.[6] These men, but especially Yoshikawa, sent information of incalculable value to the Japanese.

The other controversial matter is to what extent the Emperor of Japan was privy to the warlike preparations. An impressively-documented book, *Japan's Imperial Conspiracy* (1971), by David Bergamini, argues that not merely was the Emperor perfectly aware of what was going on, but that he was in fact the master-mind behind the whole business. From what we know of the Emperor's career and temperament, this view would appear to be a gross overstatement. It seems clear that, in October 1941, the Emperor, having summoned the Privy Council and leaders of the armed forces, ordered them not to get involved in war, and Grew, whom Mr Bergamini thinks to have been deceived all along, recorded in his diary entry for 30 September 1941 that 'we know that the Emperor had long ago told his ministers that, whatever policy they pursued, they must on no account get Japan into war with either' Britain or America.[7] Granted, when the Conference of 1 December pronounced in favour of war, the Emperor concurred, and all the main operations were reported to him as head of the State. He certainly knew as much about what was going on on his side as Roosevelt did on the

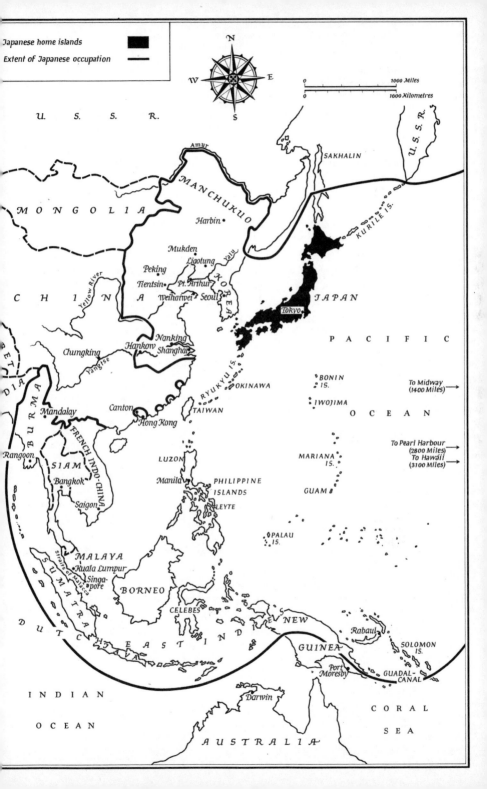

Japanese home islands
Extent of Japanese occupation

N
W E
S

0   1000 Miles
0   1000 Kilometres

U. S. S. R.

Amur

MONGOLIA

MANCHUKUO

SAKHALIN

U.S.S.R.

Harbin

Mukden

KURILE IS.

Peking
Liaotung
Tientsin
Pt. Arthur
Weihaiwei
Seoul

KOREA

Yalu

CHINA

Yellow River

Chungking
Hankow
Nanking
Shanghai

Yangtse

TOKYO

JAPAN

PACIFIC

BONIN
IS.

To Midway
(1400 Miles)

IWOJIMA

OCEAN

RYUKYU IS.
OKINAWA

TIBET
DIA

BURMA

Mandalay

Canton
Hong Kong

TAIWAN

To Pearl Harbour
(2800 Miles)
To Hawaii
(3100 Miles)

Rangoon

FRENCH INDO-CHINA

SIAM

Bangkok

Saigon

LUZON

Manila

PHILIPPINE
ISLANDS

LEYTE

MARIANA
IS.

GUAM

PALAU
IS.

MALAYA

Kuala Lumpur
Singapore

BORNEO

Straits of Malacca

SUMATRA

DUTCH EAST INDIES

CELEBES

NEW

GUINEA

Rabaul

SOLOMON
IS.

Port
Moresby

GUADAL-
CANAL

JAVA

INDIAN

OCEAN

Darwin

AUSTRALIA

CORAL

SEA

other. This does not mean, however, that he was enthusiastic about the war. All the evidence suggests that he was not.

Although the attack on Pearl Harbor dominated the world's headlines, Japan's operations elsewhere, which began almost simultaneously, were no less successful. She launched a concerted attack on Wake, Guam, the Philippines and Hong Kong. All these places fell after brief fighting, except for the Philippines, where the American resistance at Bataan and Corregidor was bitter and prolonged. Another serious loss to the Allies was the sinking within a few minutes off Colombo of the two British battleships *Repulse* and *Prince of Wales*. For a while, it seemed that Japan's 'crusade' in South-East Asia and the Pacific was proceeding even better than had been planned, and that the dream of capturing Australia and even of linking up with Germany would be realized. For the whole of Malaya was captured in January, Singapore, taken from the rear, in February, the Dutch East Indies – an especially rich prize – in March, and Burma at the end of April.

Even so, the Japanese, like Hitler's Germany, failed to appreciate the resilience and tough morale of the Allies. A sign of the spirit of defiance came with Colonel James Doolittle's token bombing of Tokyo in April 1942, because the planes had been launched by ships which had approached nearer to Japan than had been thought possible. Then a Japanese reverse of formidable dimensions occurred with the battles of the Coral Sea and of Midway Island. In previous engagements, despite the havoc caused to the Allies, the Japanese under Admiral Nagumo had suffered the loss of not a single ship. With the occupation of Midway Island, and if possible of the western Aleutians, it was hoped that a barrier could be established from the extreme north to Port Moresby in the south, across which American forces could venture only at great cost. A Japanese presence at Midway might also serve to bring out the rest of the American fleet from Pearl Harbor under Admiral Nimitz; and with this fleet destroyed, America's hope of an effective counterattack at sea would have vanished, perhaps for ever.

On 8 May 1942, the two forces joined battle. The battle of the Coral Sea was the first carrier engagement in history. From the beginning things went badly for the Japanese. Fighters sent up the night before had been severely mauled by the Americans, and some, lost in the dark, tried to land on a carrier which turned out to be the

Yorktown. In the battle itself, which was over in a morning, the Japanese suffered great losses; and although the Americans lost the *Lexington*, and the *Yorktown* in the great battle of Midway a month later, the Japanese long-term plans were permanently put out of order. They had failed, for the first time, in an invasion, and the proposed attack upon Port Moresby had at least to be deferred. Unable or unwilling to grasp what had happened, the Japanese published the story that they had gained dramatic naval victories. Indeed, it was announced after the battle of Midway that they had secured 'supreme power in the Pacific'. The Americans, exultant and with better reason, laid claim to the same achievement. Only gradually did the Japanese people grasp what had happened.

With the invasion and defence of Guadalcanal, the base on the Solomon Islands, the Americans for the first time showed themselves more than a match for the Japanese in jungle warfare. Lasting six months, the campaign was a particularly brutal one, and both sides suffered from the appalling tropical conditions; but three Japanese attempts to dislodge the Americans had failed by February 1943. As to Japanese losses, they were enormous.

So much has been said about Japanese atrocities during the Pacific war and the war in South-East Asia that there is danger that the Japanese troops and their officers may be dismissed as monsters of inhumanity. Granted, the samurai ideal and the principles of *bushido* were often forgotten, and the conduct of the Imperial armies as a whole was far inferior to that displayed during the Russo-Japanese war. But in judging the Japanese, two considerations must be borne in mind. The first is that they really believed, since it was orthodox teaching, that they were a people set above others. There were militarists who declared that the Emperor was in truth the Emperor of the world, and that it was his destiny to govern the universe with the goddess Amaterasu. The rest were subject peoples. Such an attitude inevitably breeds contempt and inhumanity. Secondly, the decency of the Japanese was rarely apparent during wartime, since it manifested itself in individual acts which rarely hit the headlines, or was reflected only in letters home to anxious wives and bewildered children. Conduct of this kind became known, if at all, only after the war.

A particularly poignant case was that of Lieutenant General Homma Masaharu, who defeated General MacArthur in the first

Philippines campaign. From what we now know of his behaviour during that campaign, he acted with as much humanity as a man in his difficult position was capable of. For this very restraint he was relieved of his command, and forced to retire to Japan in disgrace. This did not prevent his being tried after the war by the Americans, and, despite protests from his defence counsel and a member of the Supreme Court, executed. While on trial, he wrote to his wife:

> Twenty years feel short but they are long. I am content that we have lived a happy life together. If there is what is called the other world, we'll be married again. I'll go first and wait for you there, but you must not hurry. Live as long as you can for the children and do things for me I have not been able to do. You will see our grandchildren and even great-grandchildren, and tell me all about them when we meet again in the other world. Thank you very much for everything.

And he wrote an equally moving letter to his children while he was awaiting death. Of his trial and execution, the member of the Supreme Court, Associate Justice Frank Murphy, wrote:

> Either we conduct such a trial as this in the noble spirit and atmosphere of our Constitution, or we abandon all pretence to justice, let the ages slip away and descend to the level of revengeful blood purges. . . . A nation must not perish because, in the natural frenzy of the aftermath of war, it abandoned the central theme of the dignity of the human personality and due process of law.[8]

In conformity with the belief in the exalted mission of Japan, and in an attempt to make the New Order or Co-Prosperity Sphere a reality, the Japanese set out to reform the countries over which they held dominion by right of conquest. In this task, which included the spread of Japanese and cultural indoctrination, they were far from successful. Under emergency conditions, they seemed to lack the art of pacification. Granted, they treated each occupied country differently. Indo-China and Thailand were left with a measure of independence. China, Burma, and the Philippines were placed under puppet regimes. Over Malaya and the Dutch East Indies and the smaller islands, military governments of a more direct kind were imposed. Even so, freedom or resistance movements gradually began to gather strength (in the Indies Sukarno had been let out of jail); and as a result, the Japanese failed in their aim to organize their new empire into a viable economic whole, let alone a cultural unity. Neither in Europe nor in the Orient did the totalitarian New Order prove a success. All it did was to lend to previously colonial countries a new sense of identity, which, after the war, asserted itself against the European powers, anxious to resume authority. Especially was this the case with the former Dutch possession which renamed itself Indonesia.

On the other hand, the emergence of freedom movements crystallized for a time in an uprush of feeling among Asians which Japan sought to capture for her own advantage. On 5 November 1944, a large conference was held in Tokyo at which the leaders of the 'independent' countries of Asia took part, including Chandra Bose, head of the Provisional Government of Free India. Prime Minister Tōjō presided. The atmosphere was highly emotional. Asia's freedom from white domination was the central theme. The Philippine puppet, José Laurel, voiced the opinion of most of those present when he declared:

United together one and all into a compact and solid organization, there can no longer be any power that can stop or delay the acquisition by the one billion Orientals of a free and untrammelled right and opportunity of shaping their own destiny. God in his infinite wisdom will not abandon Japan and will not abandon the peoples of Greater East Asia.

It is ironical to think that a year later Japan was to lie in ruins, totally defeated; but the sentiments expressed at the conference were, in the absence of Japan's leadership, to grow stronger, until after a few years the countries in question, including Indonesia (which was not present), were free and independent of their European masters.

Once the initial losses sustained by the Americans had been made good, the Japanese began slowly to realize the enormous war potential of the United States. Hope had been placed in forcing America out of the war in the first months of hostilities. When this did not happen, Japan grew apprehensive, though the people knew nothing of the truth. At the Allied Conference at Casablanca in January 1943, it was decided, though after much argument, to step up the war with Japan, and an entirely new strategy for doing so was worked out at Quebec that August. The aim was nothing less than to expel the enemy step by step from their Pacific strongholds, using the technique of 'combined operations'. It was a task that was naturally rendered easier by the Allied successes in Europe.

This campaign was attended from the first with success. The Japanese lines of communication were far too long, and the strain of reinforcing her most distant possessions was telling on her, quite apart from the havoc wrought by American submarines. As a result, Admiral Nimitz was able to attack the Marshall Islands, the Marianas, Guam, and Palau, all in the space of a few months. The Japanese resistance was ferocious, and neither side was prepared to give any quarter. There were Japanese who refused to believe that their strength was dwindling, or who failed to realize that they were defeated. An extreme case was the tenacious little man on Guam, who 'held out' for 25 years, unaware that the war was over until he was discovered in 1972. Defeat for many was unthinkable, surrender the height of shame.

The next task for the Americans was to clean up the South-West Pacific. Here General MacArthur, determined to avenge the Philippine defeat, was in command. He was as successful as Nimitz. In September 1944, he made a landing on the north coast of New Guinea. Hardly a month passed before he was in a position to attack the Philippines. In January 1945, he invaded Luzon, and by the 5th of February Manila was in his hands. The way was now open for the invasion of Japan herself. The ultimate plan was first to attack Kyushu and then to land in force on the Tokyo plain.[9]

This last objective was a peculiarly difficult one. With whatever resolution the Japanese had defended their newly-acquired territories, they would behave with fanatical bravery in protecting their homeland. The battle for Okinawa served to prove this. The Japanese were indeed desperate. Much of their manpower was pinned down in the crumbling defence of China and Burma; and in May 1945 they were deprived of the moral support of their ally, Germany. At Okinawa, suicide tactics were employed, though they had begun in the Philippines. Midget submarines and *kamikaze* aircraft endeavoured to stem the enemy advance; but they were no match for the concerted American and Allied forces. Even so, the latter suffered great losses, as the cemeteries at Okinawa prove.

Meanwhile, the air assault had already begun. In the autumn of 1944, the Americans, operating from Saipan in the Marianas, had started bombing the mainland, and with the seizure of Iwojima, one of the Bonin islands, in March 1945, these attacks were intensified. The air supremacy was so complete that a moment arrived when the entire country, its defences beaten down, was laid open to wholesale and unremitting attack. Cities, with their thousands of wooden houses, were reduced to ashes. On 26 and 27 May, Superfortresses nearly rubbed out Tokyo, strong wind fanning the enveloping flames. Of the major cities, only Kyoto was spared, owing to the pleas of an art specialist in Washington. Deprived of imports, industry began to slow down, a food shortage ensued, and prices rose to fantastic heights.

Despite the increasing misery and desolation, the ordinary man was subject to such a measure of propaganda and thought control that he still believed that his country was winning the war. The plight of the enemy was represented as a good deal worse, and an attack on Japan itself was considered to be too foolhardy a venture for him to risk. Admittedly, some politicians took a view decidedly less optimistic. Among them were Shigemitsu Mamoru and Yoshida Shigeru, both experienced diplomats, and the former premier Prince Konoe. Moreover, the navy had been making a secret study of the war situation, the conclusion of which was that Japan could not hope to emerge victorious. The idea of putting out peace feelers was not new. Indeed, early in the war, Japan made one or two moves in this direction, hoping after Pearl Harbor and the South-East Asian campaign to hold on to her gains without further struggle. There was later an attempt to contact the Allies through the Vatican. At home, a first step was to eliminate Tōjō. There were plans for his assassination, but finally he was induced to resign in favour of General Koiso Kuniaki. When the Okinawa landings took place in April 1945, Koiso too resigned. His successor was a man thought to be in favour of peace negotiations, Admiral Suzuki Kantarō.

There was still a powerful war party, headed by the minister for war, Anami Korechika, who received the support of Tōjō and the armed forces. Others considered that some accommodation could be sought with the Soviet Union, and there was even talk of sending Konoe to Russia as an Imperial envoy, with plans for a negotiated peace. Such hopes were dashed when the Allies met at Potsdam in July 1945. Here they called for the unconditional surrender of Japan, and issued plans for military occupation.

When the Allies had called for unconditional surrender of the enemy at Casablanca, the result had been a stiffening of resistance. Something similar occurred following the issue of the Potsdam Declaration. In Japan, the people and politicians felt that unity was the sole hope of preserving the country from complete disintegration. But Potsdam was followed by the most terrible visitation that Japan had yet been called upon to endure. On 6 August 1945, an atomic bomb was dropped on Hiroshima. This was followed three days later by a similar attack on Nagasaki. Between the two bombings, but hardly seeming to belong to the same category of disaster, the Soviet Union declared war.

The effects of the nuclear bombardment of Japan – and despite the stockpiling of bombs of much greater power by five nations, Japan remains the only country to have suffered such attack – are difficult to calculate because they are still continuing. On that first morning, the world entered upon a new age. The number of deaths at Hiroshima is still a matter of dispute: Japanese sources put it at 120,000, other experts at much less. About 90,000 people survived the holocaust, *hibakusha* as they were called, and these suffered various psychological effects such as 'psychic closing off' or 'psychic numbing'.[10] Although it is probable that more people were killed in the fire-raids on Tokyo than in Hiroshima and Nagasaki, the atomic raids would seem to have affected the Japanese psyche in a new and special way. For the horror of the attacks was precisely the appearance of a new sort of pollution in the form of radioactivity. To a people so 'pollution conscious' as the Japanese, this was peculiarly abhorrent. It is possible that this has been the enduring effect of the bombings, and that the nation is still in some degree suffering from the shock.

After the atomic attacks and the rapid Russian advance over Manchuria, there was no alternative but to sue for peace. Disputes arose as to whether to accept unconditional surrender or to hold out for terms. As was to be expected, the war party, consisting of the minister for war and the chiefs of staff, were all for hard bargaining. On 9 August, at midnight, the Emperor declared that the Allied ultimatum should be accepted on condition that his own sovereignty were to be maintained. The next day this decision was communicated to the Allies through the Swiss representative. As the answer made no mention of the Emperor, another bitter argument followed. Finally, after further intervention by the Emperor, Japan agreed to accept the Allied terms, but again with the proviso that the Emperor system should be retained.

The next problem was how best to break the news to the people. It was agreed that the Emperor should deliver a broadcast message. At the last minute, the war party made an effort to prevent him doing so. Some officers of the war ministry and of the General Staff went so far as to raid the Imperial Palace in order to try to confiscate the script. They were unable to find it. A last desperate gesture was the setting fire to the prime minister's house, and that of the president of the Privy Council, two residences which had not suffered from the raids. This was to no avail. Perceiving that their cause was lost, the war minister and a number of others committed suicide.

The Emperor's broadcast was unique. It was the first time Hirohito had talked on the radio; and as he spoke his own 'sacred' Japanese, many people could not easily understand what he was saying. In fact, the message was carefully and subtly worded. 'The war', declared the Emperor, with a degree of meiosis almost calculated to raise a smile, 'has developed not necessarily to Japan's advantage.' It was obligatory for the sake of Japan and, in view of the new weapon, for the cause of civilization, to lay down arms, even though this meant having to 'bear the unbearable' and 'suffer the insufferable'. The message had a profound effect upon the people. The Emperor having spoken, there was no question but to do as he ordered. Even so, the prospects, especially the immediate ones, looked dark. As propaganda had represented the enemy to be barbarians of the vilest kind, the population cowered indoors for the first few days, while American and other personnel poured into the country. This was the first time Japanese soil had been successfully occupied, at least since that distant day when the Japanese first arrived from whatever land or lands it might be.

It was not long, however, before the tension relaxed. Shyly, and still somewhat bewildered, the people emerged. Hitherto accustomed to the drabbest of war clothes, Japanese girls soon appeared in their kimonos. There was fraternization with the conqueror. The two peoples found much in each other to attract and to intrigue. Very soon there was a rush to the altar and the shrine, and a procession of G. I. brides to the States.

9   Rebuilding and rebirth

IT MAY SEEM PARADOXICAL that the world's largest democracy should
have preserved intact the world's oldest monarchical system, as
America decided to keep the Emperor on his throne; but in doing so,
she displayed a magnanimity and a far-sightedness such as few
conquering nations have exhibited. As to the Occupation itself, it
was naturally not without blemish. Isolated outrages were committed,
and serious mistakes were made, but the press did not publish details
of incidents involving American forces. Japan was spared the extremes
of humiliation which most occupied countries have experienced.
And in General Douglas MacArthur, towering above the Nipponese
crowd, she found once more her Shogun.

For MacArthur, fresh from his Pacific victories, was appointed
Supreme Commander for the Allied Powers (SCAP). In practice,
this meant the United States, though all the Allies were represented
on a body called the Far Eastern Commission sitting in Washington,
and the only other people directly at work in Japan were Commonwealth personnel, mostly Australian. Even today, when the foreigner
is travelling in the country, he is asked first of all whether he is
American, and, if not, whether he is Australian. A complex bureau-
cracy was built up, and every now and again a directive would be
issued which the Japanese government were obliged to put into
effect. The aim of these directives was above all to democratize the
State. Next, the task was thoroughly to demilitarize the country.
Japan was deprived of all her overseas territory, including the
Ryukyu islands, which covered Okinawa. The Kurile Islands went
to Russia. An international war crimes tribunal sentenced seven 'war
criminals' to hanging: these included Tojo. Individual acts of cruelty
were also punished, so that hundreds were hanged or jailed. Meanwhile, those (and there were not a few) who had opposed the war

were let out of prison. Finally, in 1946 and 1947 there was a wholesale purge of the administration, which involved the expulsion of over 200,000 persons, including a number of politicians.

If there were to be true democracy, the party system, dormant since 1940, had to be revived. The Liberals and Progressives formed a kind of Conservative party; a Social Democratic party brought together the socialists and some moderates; and a Communist party attracted those radicals whose voice had been silenced for longer than any other. Given the prevailing unease, the economic misery, and the widespread desire for a New Order, this time at home, the Communists did reasonably well at first. There were a great many smaller parties, though these counted for little. Often, like the new religions, they were the creation of one enterprising individual.

At the 1946 elections, the Liberal leader Yoshida Shigeru became prime minister, but his party gave place a year later to the Social Democrats, who gave place to Yoshida and his Liberals again, who in 1949 gained a majority in the Lower House. Yoshida remained in office for six years. Besides his record of anti-militarism, he was a politician of the old school, dynamic and shrewd, an admirer of Winston Churchill and the British. Without his authority and strong-mindedness, post-war Japan might have suffered much greater tribulation.

The new party conflict took place within the context of a new Constitution. Drawn up by the Americans, this was issued on 6 March 1946. It provided for a bi-cameral legislature, both chambers being elected; a House of Counsellors with 250 members, and a House of Representatives of 467 members. Power rested with the Lower House, which elected the prime minister. The latter was responsible to the Diet, which meant in practice the House of Representatives. If the Constitution were to be altered, a vote of two-thirds in each house was required, with a referendum to follow. As to the Emperor, he became 'the symbol of the State . . . deriving his position from the will of the people with whom resides sovereign power'.

This change in the status of the Emperor was one of the most revolutionary which the Americans brought about. Hitherto he had been a remote, semi-sacred figure, whose public appearances were rare. When he drove through the streets, curtains, even of foreign embassies, had to be drawn. Although they wished to retain the

Emperor as a symbol, the Americans were resolved that his traditional significance for the Japanese should be radically altered. Consequently, on 1 January 1946, in another broadcast, the Emperor formally denied his divinity.[1] How much difference this disavowal made in the public mind is difficult to estimate. The intellectuals had probably paid only lip-service to the idea, but the ordinary Japanese no doubt continued to entertain it in that attitude of half-belief which satisfied, as with others, their craving for the sacred and the numinous. As to the Emperor himself, he was by nature retiring, by preference a scholar, and a trifle awkward in public; but he succeeded, as a result of encouragement from his advisers in the Imperial Household Agency, in becoming 'a smiling public man', while the Empress Nagako, motherly and of great charm, helped to put the new image of the monarchy across. In the post-war world, the Emperor, and indeed the whole of the Imperial family, played a part in public life similar to that of the British Royal family; and there are strong bonds of affection between the two. Consequently, in Japan even more perhaps than in Britain, republican sentiment remains minimal.

In the Meiji era, as we recall, the country had been divided into prefectures. Under the 'American' Constitution, local government affairs became a prefectural concern, or a question for city administration. All local assemblies were to be elected. Local taxation paid for the civil service, education, and the police (a thoroughly reformed body). In the sphere of justice, the judiciary was separated from the executive. A Supreme Court was set up, the members of which were appointed by the Cabinet, and they in turn appointed the judges and kept an eye on the validity of legislation. A provision dear to MacArthur's heart was the granting of votes to women. Of this new right, the women made good use, and women's organizations, especially the Housewives' League, became a force in the land. As in the Meiji era, women were still 'socially' inferior to the men; but in the background they exercised much greater authority than is commonly supposed, holding the purse-strings, supervising home education, and advising their husbands with shrewdness and understanding.

The re-emergence of left-wing elements, and America's wish to introduce to Japan an up-to-date labour code, produced fertile soil for the formation of modern trade unions. Immediately after the war, a Trade Union Act was passed in the Diet, followed by a

Labour Relations Act (1946) and a Labour Standards Act (1947). The Japanese worker now had a right to organize, to strike (subject to the veto of the Occupation forces), and to enjoy improved conditions, with a comprehensive system of health insurance. In 1950, a General Council of Trade Unions was formed (*Sōhyō*), which began to play an important part in political life.

No less fundamental a measure was the Land Reform Act (1946). This regulated the size of holding, eliminated absentee landlords, and increased the number of owner-cultivators. The old system of paying rents in kind was discontinued. According to the New Civil Code (1948), the right of succession to the eldest son was abolished. Henceforth this right was granted equally to all. On the other hand, it was possible to renounce one's right, and many women did so for the sake of keeping family property together.

In 1951, there was an exceptionally bad harvest, and the Prime Minister, Yoshida, ordered villages to group together and to industrialize. In any case, traditional methods began to give place to wholesale mechanization, when, in 1956, Honda developed the Peasant Motor-cultivator. The sale of this handy machine was enormous, 514,000 being purchased in 1960 alone. Between 1960 and 1965 there was a decrease in the agricultural population by about 21 per cent, a pull-out from the land of 4,430,000. By reason of the labour shortage, fathers would sign contracts with their sons granting them land on condition that they agreed to stay and work on the farm. It would happen on occasion that the housewife, resolved to force her husband's hand, would arrange for their sons to pretend to 'walk out.' This usually did the trick.

For years before the war, and most intensively during the conflict, schools had been the centres of blatant nationalistic propaganda. The Americans decided to change all that. But the task they set themselves was an uphill one. Textbooks had to be withdrawn and new ones specially written. School buildings were insufficient. Teachers were in short supply. It was now proposed to institute nine years of compulsory education, of which six years were to be spent in elementary schools and three in a middle school, which was co-educational. Three more years could be devoted to preparing for the university, making a pattern of 6:3:3.

Whether the new system, in inspiration American, was an improvement on the old, taking into account the standard of education

113

provided, was a source of much argument. The traditional *ethos* of education was gone. The school day no longer began with a ceremonial bowing before the picture of the Emperor. The old moral teaching went : 'civics' took its place. But something of the high rate of literacy prevailed. The six years of elementary education gave the children a grounding in their language, both written and spoken, which, as has been remarked, went beyond the mere learning of speech and letters. With a 99.9 per cent attendance, the children received a form of intellectual and moral training higher than that provided in most other countries. That is why your Japanese servant can produce an exquisitely written note or map, and is able to read books of a high standard. Moreover, about 40 per cent left school at the minimum age of 15, and another 45 per cent stayed until 18, while 10 per cent went on to universities. For Britain the equivalent was: 60 per cent leaving school at 15, 30 per cent at 16 to 18, and about 7 per cent going on to higher education.

Nevertheless, those parents who wished their children to proceed to university suffered from prolonged anxiety. The aim was to enter one of half-a-dozen prestige institutions, such as the University of Tokyo, Kyoto, Keio, Waseda or Hitotsubashi. Competition was exceptionally keen. As 90 per cent of the highest posts in the country were recruited from a few such institutions, many students over-worked for what was called the 'examination hell'. In their earliest years, the burden fell chiefly on the mothers: they toiled *with* their children from an early age in order to get them into the preparatory school which would best enable them to enter the higher institution. There were many breakdowns: in 1965 the Ministry of Education stated that at least 5 per cent of students at Tokyo University, the most important of all, suffered from schizophrenia and other nervous troubles. The huge growth of Parent-Teacher Associations was the result of this preoccupation with university entrance. There are today about 46,000 such associations, with a membership of nearly 18 million. Many of the associations are in reality large women's clubs, to which single women may belong.

More recently there has been a shift in educational attitudes to a more conservative position. In 1963, the Ministry of Education put forward for consideration a series of precepts which, it was claimed, exemplified the qualities of the Ideal Japanese. The programme, which was intended for adoption in schools, met with sharp opposition, as was to be expected, from the left-wing Japan Teachers Union (*Nikkyōso*). It was of a lofty idealism, advocating honesty, clean living, love of one's neighbour, patriotism, and in particular love and reverence for the Emperor. Although, with obvious qualifications, the programme might have been put forward in Yamato times, or at any time after the introduction of the Buddhist teaching, its framers claimed to be inspired not merely by traditional Japanese practice, but by modern Western educational thought and Western leaders, including John F. Kennedy (a great hero in Japan). It was an example of that syncretism to which the Japanese are prone; but with its stress on patriotism and love for the Emperor, it was basically and fundamentally Japanese. Translated into terms appropriate to Britain and the United States, the programme would have sounded strangely and almost embarrassingly old-fashioned; yet no one could claim that present-day Japan, with its enormous economic power and prestige, is a nation with an out-of-date or unsophisticated mentality. On the contrary, Japan might be said to be in many respects psychologically in advance of some of the Western democracies.

It is too early to judge the extent to which school education in Japan has become more traditional-minded. So far as university education is concerned, there is a long record of radicalism, stretching from Marxism to Anarcho-Syndicalism. After 1967, this exploded, simultaneously with comparable movements abroad, in a storm of 'protest'. In the country's hundreds of universities, much energy was consumed in violent confrontations between various left-wing factions; and the result was that a number of institutions, both state and private, were closed down.[2]

Although the protest crystallized chiefly round the war in Vietnam, the prolonged and almost hysterical demonstrations served to suggest a more profound *malaise*, though the activities of dedicated agitators, liberally endowed with funds, must not be underestimated. Scarcely less responsible for the agitation, perhaps, was the existence of a 'psychic vacuum' as a result of disillusion with traditional beliefs, and the need to satisfy an otherwise starved youthful idealism. The more violent agitation has passed, but the psychic need is still there to be satisfied.

In the 'American' Constitution of 1946, there was a clause concerning the renunciation of war. Indeed, all Japan's military installations had been dismantled, and her army, navy and air force disbanded. Shipbuilding was forbidden, and so was atomic power. Within a few years, however, the situation in the Far East underwent a marked change. By 1949, the Communists had gained control of the whole of China, and the following year war broke out in Korea. The position of the United States was a difficult one. She needed Japan as a base for operations, as a factory for arms and munitions, and as an ally. For this reason, the ban on military forces was modified, so that Japanese personnel, consisting of a National Police Reserve 75,000 strong, were able to take over the internal defence of the country. Despite the no-war clause and the ban on military bases, this Police Reserve developed, with American encouragement and to the gratification of right-wing politicians, into something like a fully-fledged army, navy, and air force.

Meanwhile, as an earnest of American desire to treat Japan as an ally and therefore no longer as a conquered nation, a peace treaty was signed in San Francisco in September 1951 and ratified in March 1952. The signatories were all those who had participated in the Pacific war, with the exception of India, China, and, most significantly, Soviet Russia. Although the occupation was at an end, occupation forces remained on Japanese soil, for the peace treaty was accompanied by a security pact according to which America, for her own sake and for the protection of Japan, was to maintain bases there.

In October 1952, seven months after the peace treaty with America, no less than 130 purged deputies (there had been further purges in 1949 and 1950, directed chiefly against the Communists) were re-elected to the Diet. These now made up 30 per cent of the new Assembly. The body was now predominantly a conservative one, and conservative it was thereafter to remain, despite shifts of emphasis. In 1955, a Liberal-Democratic party was formed by a merger, and this party continues in office at the time of writing.

The country which caused Japan most trouble was the Soviet Union. Russia was in possession of both southern Sakhalin and the Kurile Islands, so that Japanese fishermen were unable to gain access to one of their most important fishing grounds. Russia also blocked Japan's admission to the United Nations. After difficult and prolonged negotiations, the two countries came to an agreement upon diplomatic representation, and Japan's entry into the United Nations was no longer held up by veto; but upon the retention of the islands, Russia continued to be adamant.

In the case of China, Japan was in a quandary. As an ally of the United States, she could not enter into diplomatic relations with the People's Republic, but she earnestly wanted to open commercial relations. Slowly, the limitations on 'trading with the enemy' were eased, and Japanese business missions visited China with increasing frequency. Meanwhile, she enjoyed full relations with Taiwan, whither the nationalist Chinese under Chiang Kai-shek had repaired on the Communist take-over of the mainland.

Having gained her independence of America, Japan began to grow restive about the conditions which still bound her to that country. Among the young people, the students above all, and within the Socialist party, from which a small group of Democratic Socialists had split in 1959, there was mounting discontent about the presence of American bases, and in particular of nuclear weapons. When Prime Minister Kishi Nobusuke signed a new agreement in Washington in 1960, this discontent boiled over, though Kishi's aim had been to enable Japan to exercise some control over America's military policy in Japan. The new bill came before the Diet in April, and thousands of students demonstrated outside the building. Equally incensed, the Socialist party decided to boycott the House. In order to celebrate the ratification, President Eisenhower had planned to pay a visit to Tokyo; but the public turmoil was so great that the Japanese government, though acutely embarrassed, informed the President that it were best for him not to come. This was the measure of youthful feeling against the enemy-turned-ally. The Diet ratified the agreement, and so did America, though Kishi felt bound to resign.

Kishi's successor, Ikeda Hayato, triumphed in the next election, which was held in November. To some observers, this came as a surprise; but despite the student turmoil, the bulk of the Japanese people were behind the general policy of the government. And for a very good reason. Despite the hard post-war years, when the ordinary citizen suffered many privations, the morale of the nation had been such as to encourage a spirit of hard work and determination to repair the damage of the past. With the Korean war, a great opportunity presented itself of which the Japanese took immediate advantage: for the United Nations forces needed material aid quickly and on a vast scale. Moreover, America alone, in effecting 'special procurement', injected $2,200 million into the country between 1951 and 1953. This set the Japanese economy going, and very soon its growth rate began to astonish the world. In 1951, the rate was 12.2 per cent, in 1952 13.5 per cent, and, despite a recession in 1954, the figure had reached 17.9 per cent in 1959. Between 1954 and 1962, there was a doubling of real income per head, and this growth has continued.[3]

In 1964, there occurred an event which meant a great deal to the Japanese people. The Olympic Games were held in Tokyo. In order to prepare for them, the road system of the capital, never very efficient, was transformed, and sweeping fly-overs and underpasses altered the aspect of the city, now the largest in the world. There was a 'clean up', not perhaps strictly necessary, of some of the pleasure districts; and in order not to offend foreign susceptibilities, some already sufficiently sexless nude statues were encased in straw. A number of excellent hotels had been built to accommodate the thousands of foreign visitors. Many handbooks and pamphlets in remarkable 'Japanese English' were published, and some fine exhibitions of Japanese art were organized. The whole country, not just Tokyo, was on display. From the moment the Emperor announced the opening of the Games, all went with perfect precision: never had a world event been better organized. On the morrow of the Games, the mood of the country had perceptibly changed. There was a surge of self-confidence. Japan had been re-admitted, as it seemed, to the comity of nations. It had been a long and hard road back. Only those on the spot were in a position to understand how real the psychological transformation had been.

The Osaka Exhibition of 1970 confirmed the impression that Japan was now a great and dynamic force in the world, the leading nation of Asia and potentially the greatest economic power in the world. There were some who, while admiring her advance, deplored the materialistic values which seemed to underlie it. The question therefore arose, what sort of country was this New Japan, and what sort of life did its citizens lead? The last two chapters attempt to provide an answer to these questions.

10   The economic miracle

FIRST, the great economic change that has swept the country. Briefly, what is the secret of this 'miracle', described by one observer as 'the most spectacular rise in economic power and living standards the world has ever seen'?[1] When it is considered that Japan possesses almost no raw materials, and that her industries were almost all destroyed at the end of the last war, the progress of the recent decades requires explanation. For Britain, too, lost an empire after the war; and despite the Commonwealth links, it must be admitted that her recovery, after victory, has been much less impressive than that of Japan, after defeat.

One important contrast between Britain and Japan is that Japan still possesses a peasantry, whereas that of Britain disappeared as a result of the agricultural revolution of the eighteenth century. Consequently, Britain imports about half her food, whereas Japanese agriculture provides both the staple food and much else besides. Between the industrial sector and the agricultural sector in Britain there is no marked division: agriculture is virtually part of industry. In Japan the difference between the sectors is still very great. This duality extends to other spheres. There is a high-productivity sector and a low-productivity sector, with a consequent disparity in income.

Another striking difference is that between the power of trade unions. In Japan, there are enterprise or company unions rather than national unions. There were no unions at the end of the war, since they had been suspended in 1937: but the Americans ordered their reintroduction as a 'democratic measure'. As a result, the number of enrolled members grew in a short space of time from nought to 5 million. Dominating the unions were many who had been imprisoned during the war for their left-wing views. This meant that revolutionary ideas soon affected the union members; and the

Americans, alarmed, put a brake on their activities. Thereafter radical agitation was not quite so extreme; but the national union organization, *Sōhyō*, encourages every year a 'spring offensive' of wage demands. Meanwhile, the company unions agitate for bigger bonuses and fringe benefits. Unlike unions in Britain, they do not lay down the law about demarcation rules concerning who shall perform a particular job. This task is as a rule left to management. There are numerous disputes. Unions in Japan are growing more powerful; but because they do not as a rule operate on the national scale, their ability to paralyse the economy is much less great than in Britain. An exception is the mining union organization in Hokkaido, where some years back a dispute shut down the industry for 22 months, with much militant picketing. Today, there are more than 50,000 unions with nearly 10 million members. The percentage of organized labour is 36.3 per cent, as against 43.6 per cent for Britain. The total labour force in 1971 was 51,780,000 (7,680,000 in agriculture and 43,470,000 in other employment).

The tremendous work potential of the Japanese people has sometimes been ascribed to the fact that they live under a paternalistic system. Hence their loyalty to their firms is absolute.[2] While the first statement is still true, the second needs qualification. Employees shift from job to job much more frequently than in the past. Secondly, the paternalism of Japanese industry is not in reality so deep-seated in tradition as is sometimes supposed. In the days of the early factory system in Japan, there was much shifting from job to job. It was in order to prevent this flux that the employers introduced the benevolent welfare services which are so characteristic of Japanese industry today.

Certainly, the sense of corporate enthusiasm remains very strong. The 'hymns' sung before work begins, with their combination of idealism and aspiration towards greater profits, must be unique to Japan.[3] Many up-and-coming men spend part of their leisure time considering ways in which they can improve some technique or procedure in their industry. And the general atmosphere of factories is one of intensive, dedicated activity. It is this unified, determined, unremitting 'drive' which accounts for much of Japan's industrial progress.

In consequence, the old idea that the Japanese workman is poorly paid and exploited must be abandoned. This may have been true of the past. It is no longer so. Wages may still be low, but by and large the ordinary worker is as well off as his European counterpart. And his prospects, if things continue as before, are brighter. In 1971, monthly wages of regular workers averaged £105.87 (or around $254), a rise of 14.5 per cent over 1970.[4]

In Japan, the civil service is much more closely related to industry than in other countries. The Ministry for International Trade and Industry (MITI) is an organization to which there is no parallel in Britain or America. It supervises, so to speak, the entire economy, while one of its organs, the Japan External Trade Organization (JETRO), is concerned with studying the economies of other countries.[5] Thus civil servants will undertake special surveys on behalf of industry; and the government, through these and other organizations (such as the Economic Planning Agency, a dependency of the prime minister's office), will periodically order a reorientation of the economy, but always with the special aim of raising the standard of living. In MITI's 'administrative guidance', industry can be directly influenced.

> The Japanese will always tell you, especially if they assume you to be an American, that theirs is not a planned economy. In the socialist sense of the term, it is not. But Japan, even more than France, is the land of indicative economic planning *à outrance*. . . . One has only to look into the economics and statistics departments of any of its government departments or agencies: huge factory-like rooms, with economics graduates sitting row upon row, all hammering out on their adding-machines the indicative economic statistics of the New Japan.[6]

Such planning, even down to minute detail, has always been a characteristic of the Japanese form of government, from the time when the Shogun 'planned' the *daimyo* system, and conspicuously from the Meiji era, when Japan's statesmen drew up a programme of thorough Westernization.

Just as the civil service is able to draw upon the best graduates from the few select universities out of the 70 or 80 universities in the metropolis alone, so, when these men have reached early middle age, they often leave the service and take positions in big business concerns. This is a system of great value. It means that industry is able to recruit men who are familiar with government and with government planning. Hence there is little or none of the suspicion engendered against 'bureaucrats', which some other industrial systems entertain. Civil servants are regarded as men engaged in work valuable to industry, and potential recruits to industrial concerns.

Nor is the research undertaken by MITI merely a matter of theoretical exercise. The ministry runs laboratories concerned with textiles, mechanical engineering, and chemicals. It has a design centre; it runs inspection institutes, consultant services, and a patent office; and it has built one of the largest computers in the world.

Japan's economic success story may be said to begin with the steel industry, which is after all the basis of heavy industry itself. The war placed this industry in great jeopardy, as the supply of raw materials was severely restricted. After the war, the cost of importing these materials from even greater distances grew very high; but because of the enormous home demand, the industry soon began to make progress. Modern techniques were quickly assimilated: the use of oxygen for removing impurities was learnt from the USA, and later its use in the special Austrian LD (Linz and Donawitz) method was adopted. Powerful companies such as Yawata, Fuji, Nippon Kokkan, Sumitomo Metal Industries, Kawasaki Steel and the Kobe Steel Works, together with a variety of smaller companies, all in competition with one another, soon impelled the Japanese steel industry forward at a rate faster even than that of the Soviet Union. Huge ships were built to import the raw materials (coal from the United States, and iron ore from India or Australia); and in order to reduce the distance between the harbours and the blast furnaces, many of the steel plants, such as the Yawata Steel Works at Kitakyushu and the Fuji Iron and Steel Company at Kamaishi, were established in coastal regions, or, where space was insufficient, on land recovered for the purpose. The result was a considerable reduction in capital costs; Japan's production of steel per square metre soon became far greater than that of Britain and America. In order still further to offset the cost of importing raw materials, the Japanese steelmakers kept down running costs. To this end, research was undertaken by government departments (though there was no question or prospect of nationalization), in the factory laboratories, and not least in universities. Japan's steel production is now the third largest in the world, after the United States and the Soviet Union. Production in 1971 was

88,554,700 tons of crude steel. This was a reduction in fact of 5.1 per cent from 1970, but it was the first decline since 1962. Steel exports amounted to 24,178,000 tons, an increase of as much as 34.5 per cent.[7]

Whereas Japan is for the moment the third largest steel producer, she is the world's first shipbuilder. By 1945, her shipyards had been reduced to dust, her tonnage was mostly sunk, and the Americans had decided that the industry should not be allowed to revive. This interdict was lifted at the time of the Korean war; and by 1956 the Japanese had already drawn ahead of all other countries, just as now they seem likely soon to produce more ships than all the rest of the world put together.

When the ban on shipbuilding was removed, Japan did not start from scratch. She had the know-how acquired during the war, and she profited from post-war American experience, not least on account of the fact that an American company, the National Bulk Carrier Corporation, had leased the great shipyard at Kure. Two associations helped to promote development: the Maritime Association, established in 1900 and now recognized as a registration agency on a par with Lloyds and the American Bureau of Shipbuilding, and the Shipbuilding Association, established in 1897, which was devoted to technical research. There is a constant attempt to keep down costs: two advantages in particular are the comparative cheapness of Japanese steel, and the proximity of the steel plants to the yards, to which reference has been made.

Japan has an interest in building big ships, as this is the cheapest way of bringing necessary raw materials to her shores. Of recent years, she has specialized in building tankers of 300,000 tons, and bulk carriers. In 1971, the leading eight Japanese shipbuilders – Ishi-kawajima-Harima Heavy Industries, Mitsubishi Heavy Industries, Hitachi, Mitsui, Kawasaki, Nippon Kokkan, Sasebo, and Sumitomo – produced 205 ships, totalling 9,880,000 gross tons. This was roughly twice the 1956 figure, *when Japan was already in the lead.* And there is no reason to suppose that the present pre-eminence will not continue. According to Lloyds Register of Shipping, almost half the merchant ships launched in the world in 1971 were built in Japan. It is also worthy of note that, after Peru, Japan is the largest fishing nation, her total catch in 1971 being 9,300,000 tons.

To pursue this account of spectacular advancement: Japan is at present the world's largest producer of motor cycles and bicycles. A visit to towns in South-East Asia is a constant reminder of Japan, as the streets mill with Japanese two-wheeled vehicles. Japan's manufacture of these models in 1971 amounted to 3,400,402, which was an improvement of 15 per cent over 1970. Honda motor cycles, now a familiar sight everywhere, were exported to the tune of 1,304,600, an increase of 18 per cent. In the case of the motor car, however, Japan was comparatively late in the field; but after 1966, she turned her attention to car production, and already she leads the world after the United States.

Increasing car production has necessitated the construction of new and better roads. (A great encouragement to road-building, as already noted, was the Olympic Games of 1964.) Consequently, many of the large towns have been transformed by new road works, though much still remains to be done, even in Tokyo itself. There is a race between domestic car usage and highway construction. Indeed, the transition stage has seen a great increase in accidents, the rate of which is supposed to be the highest in the world. This is a record of which Japan cannot be proud.[8]

Passenger car production went up 17 per cent in 1971 over the previous year, Toyota ranking first in production as a whole (third in the world), with 1,955,033 vehicles, an increase of 20 per cent, followed by Nissan, Toyo Kogyo, Mitsubishi, Daikatso Kogyo, Honda, Suzuki, Fuji, Isuzu, and Hino. In 1967, Toyota had produced 81,000 vehicles, whereas Hino, at the end of the list, produces more than half as much now.[9] As yet, domestic car registration is only 2,915,950; and with a population of more than 100 million, and growing affluence, this figure is bound to undergo considerable increase. Indeed, it is anticipated that there will be 30 million cars on the road by 1980.

One car firm which survived the war was, interestingly enough, situated in Hiroshima. This was Toyo Kogyo. From 1931 it had specialized in small cars, three-wheelers mostly; but after 1960, it began to produce larger vehicles with its eye on the export market. Today, the Mazda 1500 saloon competes very favourably with European cars, which is why Toyo Kogyo is third on our list. By contrast to the three-wheelers designed for the narrow streets of pre-war provincial towns, the Mazda 1500 can accelerate up to a maximum of almost 100 m.p.h. It is a direct answer to Italy's Fiat 125 and Alfa Romeo Giulia.[10] Toyo Kogyo doubled its exports during the credit squeeze of 1964–65, and it may well move further up in the coming years.

In comparison with Europe, America and even Russia, Japan was late in developing her railways. She began to construct the system in the year of the Meiji Restoration of 1868, and by 1926 she had a widespread network. Indeed, so great was her progress that, in the 1930's, twelve Japanese experts were sent to the Soviet Union to reorganize the railways there. At a time when railways elsewhere are losing money and being declared obsolete, Japan has embarked upon further expansion in this sphere, and the New Tōkaidō Line between Tokyo, Osaka and Okayama is among the finest railways in the world. The author rode on the first train to take members of the public. The speed of 125 m.p.h. was achieved with smoothness, if with a slight compression of the ears (later eliminated); today, 150 m.p.h. is attained without the smallest discomfort.

Railway construction in Japan presents numerous problems. On account of the extensive mountainous areas, many tunnels have had to be constructed. Then, because of the island chain, submarine tunnels have been necessary, the most important being that linking Honshu and Kyushu by means of the Shimonoseki-Moji tunnel, completed in 1944. But on the whole, Japan, with its narrow coastal strips and mountain valleys, has proved eminently suitable for railways; and there can be few countries which are embarking upon a major programme of road expansion and railway expansion at the same time. Moreover, besides the Japan National Railways, there are privately-owned and municipally-owned railways, all of which compete vigorously for custom. In Japan, as in no other country and least of all the United States (where the railroads are fast becoming obsolete), railway travel preserves something of the glamour of the old days. On entering the carriage, the ticket inspector bows and doffs his cap, while girls distribute hot towels, and, apart from the restaurant and buffet, there is a constant sale of refreshments up and down the train. A telephone service to the main towns enables business men to keep in touch with their offices. Meanwhile, technical improvements are being constantly developed. It is hoped soon to develop a 'pendulum train' which will be able to negotiate bends without loss of speed. The first will run on the Nagoya–Nagano line in 1973.

Another industry which has prospered enormously in post-war Japan is that of petrochemicals. An industry with a production of only £11 million in 1958 had risen to £240 million by 1964. The 1971 figure was up 7 per cent on the previous year; and although this was the lowest in the history of the industry, because of a fall in demand, the general progress in the chemical industry as a whole has been most impressive.

The triumphant tale could be continued, for chemicals cover a wide field: Japan is now the chief producer of synthetic leather. And the tale continues likewise in other industries – in electronics, cameras, aircraft and space technology. As a result, Japan has built up her financial strength to a degree which in the aftermath of the war would have been thought inconceivable. At present, after Germany, she is the largest holder of foreign exchange reserves.

In 1971, Japan was severely hit by America's import surcharge. It was feared in Europe that on account of this measure and the Japan–US textile agreement, an attempt would be made, as in the past, to flood Europe with cheap Japanese goods. With a sense of responsibility, however, Japan took account of the danger, which, if allowed to spread, might well have resulted in a bitter trade war. Accordingly, Keidanren, the equivalent in Japan of the Confederation of British Industry, announced: 'We intend to move away from the excessive emphasis of the past on export volume in favour of a policy of orderly marketing.' While such a declaration was somewhat vague, Japan's actions spoke louder than words: there was, for instance, a voluntary restriction on Japan's steel exports to Europe. Moreover, the Liberal Democratic (government) party, at its 1971 annual convention, declared that its new aim was 'the elevation of national life . . . national conversion from a policy of Gross National Product to one designed to step up national welfare'. The budget for 1972 reflected this new spirit. Apart from emphasis on business recovery, the aim was to improve the standard of life by devoting large sums which would 'directly contribute to the people's welfare', such as an increase of 26.4 per cent to finance housing, sewerage and public parks, and 22.1 per cent for the introduction of new social security measures, including free medical care for all people over 70, increased old age annuities, and (incidentally) improved pensions for war veterans. Thus the picture of Japan as a gigantic business enterprise concerned only with the making of profits needs to be drastically modified. Above all, Japan intends to be one of the first in the field in fighting pollution; there is a proposal to include a 'pollution crime' in the penal code. Already some industries, e.g., paper and zinc, are lowering their production owing to the pollution caused.

As to population, there was an expansion of 34 per cent in 1947, which went down to 11.1 per cent between 1960 and 1965. It is expected that the rate may be 6.2 per cent between 1972 and 1975. The total population is now 104,539,680. Women outnumber men by 1,390,884. Of this total, 54 per cent live in urban areas (in 1960 the figure was 43.7 per cent). The size of the family is the lowest ever recorded, namely, 3.48. Japanese practise birth control widely, and Japan was a pioneer of the loop and the rhythm methods. The abortion rate is very high. Abortion on health grounds was legalized in 1948, and the act was later liberalized.

A final word regarding economic questions must be said about Japan's efforts towards economic co-operation, especially with the countries of South-East Asia. In 1970, Japan became the second largest supplier of capital resources to the developing countries of the world, thereby exceeding the aid provided by France and Germany. In fact, 'aid had now come to be regarded as an integral part of Japan's Asian policy'.[11] She has thus not only made full material reparation for her war depredations in the entire former theatre of war, but she has devoted a substantial part of her wealth to rehabilitation over and above such compensatory action. It remains to be seen whether her aggressive pursuit of markets will lead her towards an imperialism in the economic domain parallel to that which she formerly exercised under military hegemony. The signs are that she has learnt her lesson.

Just as Japan has modified her economic policy to conform with world conditions and needs, so she has adopted a new stance in her foreign policy. After the war, she was naturally obliged to conform to American wishes, and after the ending of the occupation she deliberately adopted a policy of 'low posture'. With the increasing power of China, however, she has realized the need to assume a more positive position. Her dilemma is that, for the present, having no atomic weapons, she is obliged to shelter under America's 'nuclear umbrella'; but her position following President Nixon's visit to China was not an easy one, especially in view of her close links with

Taiwan. The return of Okinawa to the homeland in May 1972 satisfied her national pride, and now she hoped to recover the Kurile Islands and the southern part of Sakhalin from the Soviet Union. Of Russia she remains as nervous as she was of China. Russia's increased presence in the Indian Ocean might well threaten Japan's oil supplies, 95 per cent of which come from the Persian Gulf through the Straits of Malacca. Whether Japan would ever manufacture atomic weapons of her own was a delicate question, though voices in favour of her doing so were more clamorous at the beginning of the seventies than they were a few years earlier. She was certainly technically capable of taking such a step.

Prosperous as never before and in some ways only at the beginning of her economic development, Japan confronted a new situation in Asia and an enlarged Common Market in Europe at the opening of 1973. What was the mood of the people occupying this dynamic archipelago? That is the final question we have to answer.

18 Against Tokyo's modern skyline, a corner of the Imperial Palace
preserves the traditional Japanese architecture.

19 *Above:* Aftermath of
the radioactive desert tha
was Hiroshima.

20 *Left:* Symbol of rebirt
Tange Kenzō's national
indoor gymnasium.

21 *Right, above:* Shintō
wedding procession.

22 *Right, below:* Zen med
tation class.

23 Grading cultured pearls - one industry in which the machine is no substitute for the skilled human hand and eye.

24 The diving fisherwomen Hekura island bring up shell fish and edible seaweed from as deep as eighty feet.

25 The intensive, dedicated drive of the Japanese worker has given Japan the world's biggest shipbuilding industry. This picture shows the launch from the Kure shipyards of the 132,000-ton tanker *Nisshō Maru*.

26 The Noh plays, by origin probably religious ceremonies, are enjoying a revival today with all classes, in spite of archaic language and formalized acting.

27 *Cha-no-yu*, or Tea Ceremony: the traditional ritual, with its carefully prescribed movements, originated as a refreshment during the concentrated effort of Zen meditation

In the north of Japan, with five months of snow, ski-ing is a mass
ort. This party of schoolchildren heading for the snow slopes reminds
e that Japan took the first three places in the ski-jumping in the
pporo winter Olympics.

11   Japanese life and thought

VISITORS TO JAPAN today remark often how great has been, for good or for ill, the Americanization of social life. They compare what the Americans appear to have done in Japan with the superficial Anglicization of the Indian sub-continent during centuries of British rule. The comparison is misleading. The 'Americanization' of Japan began as early as the Meiji Restoration. To take a minor example: baseball, played so assiduously by the Japanese, is sometimes thought to be a post-World War II innovation. In fact, it was played long before the war. Furthermore, the Japanese mentality is such that the people have an impulse, and indeed a gift, for what may be called selective assimilation: a form of borrowing which leaves their own national core intact. The student of cultural relations has much to learn from the curiously unique example of Japan. Almost it might be said that whenever Japan borrows something new, she becomes more herself. Thus she is perhaps more thoroughly Japanese today than she was on the morrow of the Meiji Restoration, when so many extravagant notions were entertained: she is certainly more Japanese than she was on the morrow of the surrender of 1945, when a peculiarly unattractive side to her character had been for so long in evidence. For it is not Japanese merely to live, dress, and sometimes to think Japanese; it is also Japanese to live, dress and sometimes to think in a foreign manner. This habit of adopting foreign ways · began at the time of the China cultural missions: it recurred at the time of the arrival of the Portuguese, when many Japanese took to dressing like the newcomers and even to wearing crosses. In other words, Japan cannot wholly revert to her past, nor can she become quite Westernized: she can attain viability only by a peculiar compromise in which the Japanese side of her character necessarily remains the stronger.

◄ 29 Seaside holidays are a problem for a nation with   137
a population of more than a hundred million.

Thus the Japanese today go to work in Western clothes, but, in the case of the men, they may change into *yukata*[1] as soon as they reach home again. This does not always refer to the young, who may wear the international uniform of roll-top sweater and levis, except perhaps after the bath. The girls have easily adapted themselves to Western dress, which they wear with grace, though the Japanese figure sometimes looks a little gawky in it, unless it be carefully tailored to disguise a flat bosom and sometimes spindly legs. At most important gatherings, the kimono is worn. This beautiful garment has neither buttons nor fasteners. It is held together by a sash called *obi*, often richly patterned. With better feeding, the height of the girls has greatly increased since the war, just as has their longevity, which has been augmented by twenty years. Those of short stature, and this still represents a large number, seek to augment their height both by high-heeled shoes and by a piled-up coiffure or a chignon liberally eked out with false hair. In this way, a girl, defying the Biblical edict, can easily add a foot to her stature. Some of the most effective hairdo's in this style are those worn by *vendeuses* or waitresses serving in cafés.

Foreigners in Japan are bound sooner or later, but sooner rather than later, to be asked what they think of the modern Japanese girl. The girl is supposed to indicate or typify the quality of a culture in a particular fashion, and this is probably accurate. Anthropologists would be better able to throw light upon the nature of the societies they study if they were to investigate this aspect rather than engaging in arid studies of kinship patterns.

Some recent novels and films have given a greatly distorted picture of Japanese womanhood, beginning with the abominable Kissy Suzuki; and there have been one or two Japanese females of international fame who are about as untypical of Japanese womanhood as it is possible to imagine. In general, it may be said that the Americanized Japanese woman is less than attractive, perhaps because the gentle and clear Japanese female voice does not easily adapt to the American accent. Moreover, the Japanese woman is not psychologically suited to taking the front place which the American woman commands as of right. This does not mean that Japanese women lack strong character. On the contrary, their strength of character is one of the most striking things about them; and, so far as we can tell, this has always been so.

In the past, Japanese women have exerted great authority. The early ruler and priestess of Ise, Princess Pimiko, must have been a remarkable woman. The Empress Jingō (200–269?) is said to have led the armies in Korea. The Empress Gemmyō (708–715) ordered the compilation of Japan's oldest book, the *Kojiki*. Then there were Murasaki Shikibu and Sei Shōnagon, both striking characters as well as writers of genius. The Mitsui Company was probably founded by a woman.[2] Women have shown extreme bravery, especially in shielding their menfolk from attack. To take two twentieth-century examples: during the attempted *coup d'état* of 1936, Viscountess Saitō, faced with her husband's assassins, said 'Kill me instead: my husband cannot be spared by the country', and put her hand over the mouth of the machine-gun pointing at them both, while, in the same incident, Mrs Watanabe, wife of General Watanabe, lay down on the floor with her husband in her arms so that the young 'patriots' were obliged to shoot under her body to kill the General. And we have spoken already of the samurai ideal, which was shared by women and men alike. During the war, the endurance of Japanese women, in however dubious a cause, was outstanding, and they have been courageous in public affairs, being especially outspoken about social evils. Finally, there have been a number of women who have played a part in leading new religious movements, one of the most extraordinary being Mrs Nakayama Miki, the founder of Tenrikyō (see p. 155).

Thus although MacArthur 'emancipated' Japanese women after the war, they were never in any sense a downtrodden sex. The woman was always 'mistress of the household' (*Oku-San*, the title still employed for wife). To quote from a modern classic still valid:

The husband was the lord of the family; but the wife was mistress of the home, and, according to her own judgment, controlled all its expenses – the house, the food, the children's clothing and education; all social and charitable responsibilities, and her own dress, the material and style of which were supposed to conform to her husband's position. Where did she get the money? The husband's income was for his family, and his wife was the banker.[3]

Indeed, the magazine *Fujin Kōron*, which has an immense circulation, made an enquiry in May 1966, which revealed the fact that in

84.8 per cent of cases the woman took sole charge of the household expenses.

In the past, women have been obliged to conform to a variety of traditional practices, in a society already noted for its stringent taboos. Until recently, and still today in some villages, she bore her child in a sitting posture, on a couch in a darkened room. For 75 days after the confinement she was pronounced 'unclean', being forbidden to visit either temple or shrine. She suckled her child up to the 109th day, when there was a festival called the 'Festival of the First Meal', at which boiled rice and broth were consumed. She carried the child on her back for many months, as a result of which Japanese children developed the capacity, which they still possess, of being able to sleep in a variety of positions. Today, it is a common sight to see Japanese asleep in public vehicles, with their tickets stuck in their hatbands.

The closeness of the child to the mother established a life-long relationship. During the war, young soldiers, in danger or about to launch an assault, found themselves, instead of calling on the name of the Emperor as was expected of them, instinctively uttering the word 'Mother!' The love between mother and child is regarded as the highest kind of love. This has led some observers to assume that the Japanese entertain no romantic feelings for one another; but so to argue is to ignore the highly sentimental side to the Japanese character, the love-suicides (though rarer than formerly), and the addiction to romantic stories and films.[4]

In the past, a married woman became very soon a matron, wearing a dull-coloured kimono; and this is still the everyday wear of the older generation. A great deal has been made of the fact that, having given her husband children, the wife then ceased to arouse the feelings that had originally brought them together, even when the marriage was an arranged one. It is true that the richer man would sometimes, indeed frequently, cultivate other attachments, including geisha; and an official with a good deal of public entertaining to do would sometimes take a 'geisha wife' to fulfil this side of his obligations. But the ordinary man neither needed nor could afford such luxuries. As to the attitude of husbands, a Japanese wife, even when taking second place to another woman, seems to command a respect and affection that is at least as strong as in Western countries.

While the 'arranged marriage' was normal in the past, it is by no means so rare today. In 1971, the Tokyo Marriage Research Centre ascertained that of 968 couples due to be married, 82 per cent were getting married for love, and the rest as a result of 'arrangement': which is quite a high proportion for these days. The marriage-broker or *Nakōdo* had always to be a married man, as his wife would play an important part in the proceedings. He never received a fee. The chief function of the go-between was to make enquiries as to health and character, and to arrange introductions. In the past, there were cases of forced marriages, usually in order to secure additional property, and dramas were written on the theme of girls who rebelled in the name of true love against such tyranny. But it is almost inconceivable that such compulsion would be exercised today. If the couple, once introduced, did not take to each other, the scheme was called off. There would seem to be a good deal to be said for such a method of testing and assessing compatibility.

On the question of sexual morals in Japan, here again the issue has been clouded by lurid Japanese films, and the antics of one or two 'international' Japanese. It would seem probable that, as the Japanese live nearer to the norm of physical existence than some other people – by which is meant nearer to Nature – their attitude to sex is less tinged with hysteria than in the case of the West, where the subject has tended to get out of hand. There is very little of what used to be called prudery. A poet and official of the fourteenth century, who later became a Buddhist priest, wrote as follows: 'A man may excel at everything else, but if he has no taste for love-making, one feels something terribly inadequate about him, rather like a valuable wine-cup without a bottom.' But the same man said, with no less authority: 'Nothing leads a man astray so easily as sexual desire.'[5] The same temperateness seems to prevail today. As Kawasaki Ichirō, a foreign-service officer, has written: 'The Japanese are not prone to promiscuity or sexual excess'.

Westerners making acquaintance with modern Japanese literature may be surprised at the preoccupation of many of the female characters with *purity*, understanding that word in a quite conventional sense. An interesting example is the novel *The Flowers are Fallen* by Shiina Rinzō,[7] with its central character, the girl Seikō, aged 18. The author received numerous letters from readers sympathizing with his heroine's search for moral perfection. Nor is it without interest that the founder of the famous Takarazuka Girls'

Opera (named from a watering-place near Osaka), a street-car magnate, laid down the strict rule: 'Be pure, correct, and beautiful.' It is not easy to imagine such an injunction being given to a group of show girls in the West, without provoking a reaction of mild cynicism.

What has just been said might be taken to suggest that Japan is the ideal country, with a population of Sun Children living in idyllic happiness and innocence. This is naturally far from being the case. If, however, Lafcadio Hearn declared that in Japan (or the Japan of his day) you have the *illusion* of living in an earthly paradise, it follows that there must be a special quality about Japanese life which promotes this curious but undeniable feeling. This has something to do with living closer than others to the norm, though admittedly the norm is difficult to define. Times are changing; and as certain Western ideas penetrate deeper into Japan, the nature of life may be modified. Students who have nothing better upon which to nourish their sensibility than the arid Marxist ideology are unlikely to end up with a view of life as serene as their fathers' – those fathers who, in some cases, during the height of the war, thought nothing incongruous in writing a string of delicate *haiku* to assuage their feelings. There are indeed signs that the women are getting restive, chiefly perhaps because of propaganda from outside. When Simone de Beauvoir's *Deuxième Sexe* was issued in Japanese translation in 1953, it rapidly sold 600,000 copies. On the other hand, we must not assume that, because a book sells well, it necessarily influences the conduct of its readers, or we should observe some peculiar results on occasion. By far the greater number of divorces are requested by women. Yet we notice in Japan a phenomenon observable elsewhere, that in public life the role of women is not necessarily increasing. In 1946, there were 39 women deputies, the fruit perhaps of the post-war emancipation. In 1947, however, this figure had dropped to 15, in 1949 to 12, in 1953 to 9, in 1955 to 8, and in 1967 to 6. (In 1967, however, there were 17 women senators.)

Certainly, in Japan there is still a marked discrepancy between the kind of life lived by men and that lived by women. The enormous entertainment world centring round bars, clubs and cabarets, which is so striking and lively a feature of each town, however small, caters exclusively for men; and this has been so at least since the Edo period. Nor is it possible for women to 'crash' this world, as they are doing in the West to men's other preserves, such as clubs and societies. If they were to do so, the entire system would collapse, for it is doubtful whether the thousands of bar-girls and hostesses would consent to entertain women along with men. There *is* a bar life, and many men find they can unwind in it as in no other way. And needless to say, much of this life is of a perfectly innocent kind, despite the affirmations of some foreign writers. Granted, some bars, and especially some cabarets, being blatantly commercial establishments, purvey all that is sordid and meretricious in a Western cabaret; and the same goes for the strip-tease booths, which must surely indicate some residual puritanism *à rebours* in their clients. But the ordinary Japanese bar, where the clientèle is habitual, fulfils a social function which, so far as the men are concerned and the women too who may find a marriage partner thereby, is psychologically beneficial.

Apart from restaurants, the only places which women may frequent as easily as men are the excellent cafés, the like of which do not exist in the West. They were established in the 1930's, to compete with the much more expensive tea-houses. Here there are waitresses called *nēsan* (literally 'elder sister'), who, after much delicate negotiation, may be 'dated', and here a boy may take his girl-friend for an afternoon or evening in conditions of comfort, relative privacy, and inexpensiveness. Here, too, a girl may easily go by herself if she has a mind to. It is one of the blessings of these cafés that alcohol may be obtained there at any time. Japan's licensing laws are among the most civilized in the world. The result is that whereas there may be a certain amount of tipsiness, there is nothing like the deliberate and compulsive drunkenness to be found in countries where drinking needs to be fitted into a rigid and often quite irrational time-table.

On the whole, therefore, the girls live a life much narrower and possibly harder than their menfolk, though this appears to worry them less than might be supposed. Japanese women do not as a rule drink to anything like the degree found among Western and certainly American women; but nor are they so bored as some of their sisters in the partially emancipated Moslem countries, who have failed so far to work out a satisfactory female way of living. Japanese girls, at least of the middle classes, seem always to be busy. After a hard day's work in an office, many of them go to classes in cooking, Tea

Ceremony or flower-arrangement; and when it is realized that a full diploma in the two latter arts may take ten years to obtain, something of the dedication of these young creatures can be imagined. So much of a girl's time is spent on these accomplishments because they are part of what is called 'preparation for marriage'. This preparation is integral to female education, and may be undertaken without there being a partner immediately in view.

Thus the leisure occupations of young men and women tend not to overlap. The young men may study judo, kendō and aikidō; but although there is a woman's judo and karate open to all, the two sexes do not learn together. Apart from the cafés and cinemas, young men and women, especially students, may meet at the drama clubs, which are popular. Family entertainments and gatherings tend to be formal, and there is much visiting and 'going out' on festival days (*o-matsuri*). Even so, there seems to be neither the slight embarrassment nor the over-heartiness in the day-to-day meeting of the sexes such as is often to be found in Western countries; and this may be due to the element of ritualism in daily life, which no amount of Westernization has succeeded in breaking down – above all the formal bowing, still carefully adjusted to the presumed rank of the person concerned. Those who inveigh against conventions do not always realize how many awkwardnesses and uncertainties their adoption overcomes.[8]

It therefore seems likely that the present position of Japan as a 'man's country', with women exercising considerable power behind the scenes, will remain unaltered for some time to come. For if the balance were to shift radically in the direction of sexual parity on the American pattern, the whole basis of Japanese society would undergo change; and there are powerful forces, not least among the women, resisting such a transformation. The assumption is made on occasion that social causes such as Women's Liberation must inevitably triumph, and that only male chauvinism prevents it from doing so; but what has grown up largely on the soil of America need not necessarily prove suitable to that of Japan. It depends what your grievances are, and it is doubtful whether *unhappiness* is one from which Japanese women notably suffer.

Granted, this does not mean that the women have no complaints about their present position in society. There are certain careers in which they have difficulty in making headway. Moreover, Japanese women seem to possess an unsatisfied zest and curiosity about the world which their menfolk appear to lack. It is the girls rather than the boys who approach the foreigner in the street and express the wish to engage in English conversation.[9] Moreover, the girls are great letter writers. The following appeared in the London *Daily Mirror* for 11 May 1968, under the heading 'Adam wanted a girl – he got 2,877': 'Adam Nichols, 17, received this number of letters in two years, and they still come in. His name was sent by his schoolmaster to a Japanese educational centre, and his name got into a pen-friend magazine.' This is not untypical. Japanese girls and women could expand their personalities more than they do; but beyond a certain point they would cease to possess the winning qualities which make them what they are. And that would be to deprive Japanese culture of one of its most attractive qualities.

Although the Japanese as a whole are not as yet particularly well housed, 97 per cent of households have TV, and 85 per cent a washing-machine and refrigerator.[10] This access of wealth, and the possession by the ordinary Japanese of a variety of consumer goods, lend to the surface of Japanese life that materialistic aspect which has frequently been remarked; but the Japanese character is such that the ordinary folk do not as yet seem to depend on this affluence for their contentment. An experienced French commentator, Robert Guillain, has written: 'The greater part of the poor and humble Japanese lead comparatively happy lives and are contented with their lot. ... [Their] needs are modest, and they correspond to [their] means.... A Japanese requires only a very slight improvement in his material well-being to derive a great pleasure from it.'[11] Such a judgment is perhaps a little bold;[12] but its truth may be gauged by comparing other Asian countries, where misery and want are written upon people's faces.

The Japanese lacks the impression of avidity, greed and predatoriness so visible elsewhere, though whether this is due to training or physical constitution is not easy to say. The richer among the Japanese do not engage in the 'conspicuous consumption' that one finds in the West, and especially in the United States. Immensely wealthy industrialists such as Matsushita Konosuke make a point of cultivating the simple life, whatever may be the scale of their official entertainment. Moreover, the Japanese temples and shrines, with an occasional exception such as the temples on Mount Kōya, do not display the magnificence of some Christian cathedrals. The Grand

Shrine at Ise still preserves the simplicity of the earliest Japanese (or Chinese) architecture, by being rebuilt in exact replica every twenty years. Moreover, the Tea Ceremony is noted for its simplicity, and for the simple if beautiful utensils, especially the tea-bowls, used in it. Finally, the Japanese house, which is thought to be of southern origin,[13] is still based upon the measurement of the *tatami* mats of 0.80 m. by 1.80 m., which was considered to be all the space an individual man needed. Half of all Japanese families still live in dwellings less than 30 square metres. Such dwellings are uncluttered; and when a Japanese, such as the late Mishima Yukio, lives in a Western-style house full of Western ornaments and *bric-à-brac*, the effect tends to be singularly oppressive. In the old days, the cleanliness and orderliness of the houses was ensured by police-supervised 'spring cleaning', undertaken sometimes twice a year, when *tatami* and paper windows were renewed, vermin exterminated, and the whole place washed down. This was necessary, because *tatami*, unless carefully tended, could become very tatty, and there was a habit of consigning rubbish under the floor of the living-room, where rats would get at it. Although the traditional wooden house is being replaced by blocks of flats, the aim is still simplicity of design.

Two Japanese habits which will take a long time to disappear are sleeping on the floor and bathing in the traditional style. Westerners often find the former difficult to get accustomed to; there is some reason to believe that the Japanese hip-bone is less prominent than in the case of other people. The bedding can be stowed away in cupboards in the daytime, which means that bedrooms can be dispensed with. Bathing was no doubt by origin a ritualistic lustration, and it still preserves this aspect. The washing is done outside the bath; then there is a long soaking in piping hot water, perhaps as much as $110°$ Fahrenheit. The bath is no less necessary to a Japanese than are eating and drinking, and it is often the prelude to both. For those who have no interior bath (usually a large wooden tank), there is the public bathhouse; and this tends to form a kind of club where the neighbours exchange local gossip. In the past, especially during the cold months in the country, the mother would keep her children in the bath up to their necks for hours at a time. Mixed bathing has long been forbidden, but there are various springs or *onsen* where it is still permitted, particularly in Hokkaido and Kyushu. The interdict may have been due to foreign influence and custom, to which at one time so much attention was paid. It is not necessarily to the good. In many modern houses the European-style bath is being installed, and this again perhaps is a tendency to be regretted. It will certainly have the effect of modifying an important aspect of Japanese culture.

Until the Meiji Restoration, the Japanese ate practically no meat. Today, Japanese meat, especially Kobe beef, is some of the best in the world. The manner of eating it is usually Western, but there are steak houses where only chopsticks are provided. Apart from steak, *sukiyaki* is the meat dish *par excellence*, consisting of sliced beef, pork, or chicken, cooked with vegetables, soy sauce, bean curd, and *shirataki*, which resembles macaroni. Part of its attraction is the way it is prepared. A little stove with a pan is placed on the table, with the ingredients stacked in dishes. The waitress or hostess manipulates these with chopsticks, and the growing aroma is a feast in itself. Unfortunately, *sukiyaki*, which is probably Western in inspiration, tends to be expensive, and the ordinary person can afford it only once in a while. As portions adapted to the Japanese stomach are usually too small for the Western one, a second helping is nearly always desired. *Sukiyaki* means literally 'hoe roast', and this is supposed to date from a time when farmers prepared the meat outside on their hoes, since meat-eating was not approved.[14]

Fish is a delicacy in Japan, and a great variety of it is eaten. Two preparations are especially favoured: *tempura*, probably in origin a Portuguese word, where the fish, usually prawns, is coated in batter and fried in sesame oil. It is eaten sitting up at a bar. Then there is *sashimi* or raw fish, usually tunny or sea-bream, which is eaten with soy sauce and spiced with horseradish, set apart to begin with like a small cone of incense. This can form a delicious meal, owing to its freshness and piquancy of taste, though some foreigners at first find the idea of eating it repulsive.

Despite these delicacies, the favourite food of the people is still rice. Indeed, the original name of Japan was *Mizuho-no-kuni*, the 'land of the fresh rice ears'. It is a sacred food, and to this day the Emperor cultivates his own rice field in his Tokyo residence. It had to be served kneeling, and cooked rice was sprinkled on the Shintō shelf.[15] The whole of the festival calendar was based upon rice-planting. The annual activity was as follows. In October, the best grains were chosen. In March, they were put into big jars of warm water, where they swelled. In April they were planted in kitchen gardens. In May, transplanting began, which was followed by a few days' holiday. Irrigation took place in June. In July, there was thinning out. Throughout August there was a constant fight against pests and birds. In September, the month of typhoons, there was perpetual anxiety. Finally, in October there came the harvest. New *sake* was brewed in December.

Of recent years, Japan has made great progress with rice production. In 1955, production per hectare was 3.8 tons, as compared with 2.2 tons in Vietnam and 1 ton in Cambodia. But after 1956, as a result of an invention by a Toyama farmer, production per hectare has risen to the high figure of 9.15 tons. Since about 73 per cent of arable land consists of paddy-fields, Japan's over-all production is therefore enormous, far in advance of most other countries, despite the comparative smallness of her territory.[16]

If rice is the sacred food, *sake* is the sacred drink. Made by breaking down rice grains with a fungus, its manufacture is a lengthy process. The drink can naturally vary greatly in quality. Some forms of *sake*, such as Nada *sake* from Nada, near Kobe, have a rich aroma. (Nada is matured in cedar casks.) At one time, vipers used to be pickled in some brands of *sake* to improve their flavour. Served warm and in small delicate cups, it has a gentle intoxicating effect. St Francis Xavier commented on the quality and effects of *sake*, remarking that the Japanese were strong drinkers. They have preserved this reputation, and it is one which they tend to identify with manliness and virility. 'Are you a heavy drinker?' is a favourite and by no means impolite question to be asked at even the most serious interview.[17]

Even so, the poorest people among the peasantry themselves who produced the rice were not always allowed, as we have seen, to eat it. It had to be paid over to the feudal lord, who distributed it in stipends. Apart from millet, the poorest often ate *kō-no-mono*, literally 'odoriferous things', which were mixed pickles or preserved vegetables. Today, these are often eaten with rice itself, adding greatly to its flavour. Wooden luncheon-boxes to be purchased on trains often contain rice, with a small compartment at the side for pickles. Another inexpensive dish is *soba*, a macaroni-like substance made of buckwheat flour, which, eaten with soup, is very warming. More expensive but extremely popular is *sushi*, which consists of rice wrapped in thin seaweed or *nori*, or raw fish with a thick rice base, like a lozenge. Very welcome after repeated draughts of *sake*, *sushi* is often served in round lacquered boxes, which, purchased independently, form suitable presents.

Up to a decade ago, such dishes were the staple of the people. Now, a more Western diet is coming into fashion: bread, eggs and milk are increasingly popular, and the average daily calorie intake is almost 2,500. This has brought about a revolution in eating habits and no doubt in health.

Despite the multiplication of Western hotels, the favourite Japanese mode of eating is still seated on the *tatami* at a low lacquered table. Foreigners are often provided with back-rests and arm-rests; but the correct posture, not always nowadays observed by the Japanese, is to sit with the legs tucked underneath. The room is barely furnished, but it has a kind of recess or alcove at one end called the *tokonoma*, which is adorned with a scroll or *kakemono* and perhaps a simple flower arrangement. There would seem to be no reason why the Japanese should not have borrowed the chair from China; but despite the popularity of things Chinese, especially in the Nara period, they did not do so. Had it been introduced, there would no doubt have been an end to *tatami* as a floor-cover, and the style of the Japanese house might have radically altered. In most Japanese *ryokan* or inns today, however, there is a table and two chairs in the window.

Food is brought on in little bowls. Soup is usually served to begin with, and there exists no taboo against sipping noisily. In the same way, by a swift manipulation of the chopticks, rice and pickles may be eaten with a rapidity, and an accompanying hiss, which the foreigner would be well advised not to seek to emulate. As to breakfast, though Western ham and eggs can be served (usually on the cold side), the traditional fare is soup of fermented beans, rice and pickled vegetables, a mixture to which it may take time to become accustomed at that hour. Japanese can eat at all times of day, and *tōfu*, made of fermented bean cakes, raw or roasted or fried in oil, is always delicious. With *sake*, a salted biscuit called *o-sembei*, often wrapped round with seaweed, may be recommended.

The Japanese are as addicted to mass sport as any other country, and they are extremely keen to engage in international competitions. They train with almost fanatical energy. In the case of a sport which they may hitherto have neglected, a deliberate effort may be made to 'put themselves on the map'. Thus in 1971 Japan had only three squash rackets courts. But by 1975 she plans to have a total of 7,000, which is more than the total in the rest of the world. In other words, Japan has 'decided to make squash a national sport'.[18] It is similar with other activities, such as bowls. Once the will is there, whether to row at Henley or to enter some other prestigious contest, the country as a whole mobilizes its energies to achieve success, and nearly always does so.

For that reason, there is a cult of sporting heroes quite as enthusiastic as in the West; but in Japan there are national sports which have no equivalent elsewhere, such as sumō. Sumō has championships in January, May and September at the Kokugikan, in Kuramae, Tokyo. It is a sport of great antiquity. The wrestlers, often six feet tall or over, can weigh as much as 400 pounds. This is brought about by a special diet and a unique training. An elaborate ritual, and gargantuan gestures or lunges precede each bout. This may last but a few minutes or even seconds, as the aim is not so much to throw the opponent as to pitch him out of the ring. Dressed in traditional costume, the referee does not permit the wrestlers to start until their breathing is as near to synchronous as possible. As the wrestlers enter the ring, naked but for an embroidered apron, they scatter salt in a purificatory gesture. Many of the audience watch from little pens, where they can eat from lunch-boxes. The enthusiasm is great, as the effort to dislodge the opponent can be prodigious. A sumō hero passing along the street will attract a throng. The wrestlers retire early, and are supposed to die young from their exertions; but in fact, many become judges or umpires, four of whom sit under the central canopy at each contest. Whereas all the Japanese martial arts, especially judo and karate, have enjoyed popularity in the West, sumō is difficult to export. There is no sign that it is losing its hold on the Japanese public – quite the contrary.

The Japanese film is famous throughout the world, and directors such as Kurosawa, Mizoguchi and Ichikawa are revered as much as their Italian and Swedish counterparts. The Japanese film industry is in fact older than that of America, for the first Japanese film was made in 1897, whereas a film called *The Great Train Robbery*, made in Pittsburgh in 1903, was the first of its kind. Japan had no silent films, strictly speaking, for there were always 'explainers', most of whom were originally trained in the *kabuki* school. The ordinary commercial Japanese film has tended to reflect the trend in the West, and Japanese directors, not to be outdone, have produced films of an eroticism and violence which can hardly go further without falling into absurdity. Educationists and bodies concerned with the public welfare have been as concerned at this trend as they are elsewhere; and there is a censorship of films in Japan which has from time to time ordered cuts in a foreign film, with the usual outcry from 'progressive' circles. A source of almost endless material for popular films, equivalent to the American Westerns, are stories of samurai warriors.

The cinema, as in other countries, has felt the threat of television. The latter became rapidly an integral part of Japanese life. With its clean contours, the 'box' somehow suits a Japanese *tatami* room better than it does many a Western one. Moreover, Japan was the pioneer of the miniature 5-inch screen television set, which can grace a bar better than the dominating and attention-monopolizing ordinary set in the English pub. Having so thoroughly immersed themselves in the 'television revolution' and having so many programmes to choose from, the Japanese are becoming more discriminating in their viewing. If, however, one glances at the screens which seem to be perpetually 'awake' in hotel lounges, one finds as often as not a samurai film in progress, though, as in the cinemas, foreign films enjoy a considerable vogue. Japan has its television 'personalities', its pop stars, and its eternal serials; but, as with sound radio, there is a paternalistic atmosphere pervading the programmes which arises from the fact that Japan is a country united in its basic ideas and principles.

On the subject of pop stars, when it comes to a new fashion or a change in vogue, the youth of Japan tends to take its cue from the West. British and American stars are household names, and the sale of their records enormous. In some respects, however, the emergence of the pop star, with his mop of hair and often bizarre garments, did not present such a novelty to the Japanese as it did to other peoples, because many Japanese, particularly students, wore a Beatle cut long before the famous group came on the scene. And it was customary with students to cultivate a dishevelled appearance. The bobbed hair with the heavy fringe is supposed to have been imitated from the Ainu. When the Beatles first visited Japan in 1966, having been preceded by several other well-known groups, the authorities took special precautions to ensure that order was maintained, and in fact the reception was, by comparison with the hysteria elsewhere, rather subdued. It was felt that Japanese youth, whatever its enthusiasm, should be on its best behaviour.

On the whole, this orderliness is observable in Japan in other group manifestations, and it may be the result of centuries of discipline. Schoolchildren spontaneously go about in groups or crocodiles, and so often do adults. The most obvious exception, however, is direct political demonstrations. Here the students, or rather the radically-minded among them, are perhaps the most violent in the world. The period between 1967 and 1969 was one of university chaos. The explanation of this uprush of violent energy is probably more involved than may at first be thought. Part of it is without doubt due to a world-wide *malaise* among young people, in consequence of a shift in values; and this would affect Japanese students in particular, because, in addition to their long tradition of radicalism, they are still suffering from the prolonged psychic shock of the war, the defeat, and the occupation. In this respect, they differ from a country such as France, which had its 'resistance myth' to sustain its shaken morale, whereas the Japanese have nothing equivalent. On the other hand, the renewed interest in the Pacific war, and the strange case of Mishima Yukio, suggest that a myth may be in the making. The Mishima suicide, that is to say, may be the beginning of a cult of national regeneration. And there is no knowing where this may lead.

Since the aesthetic sense has been so highly developed in Japan, it is not surprising that the modern Japanese should go in for the arts in a big way. Cultivation of their traditional arts is part of their way of life, but they are passionately devoted to modern art. Quantitatively, it is possible that there are more artists in Japan than in any European country: the number of registered artists in Tokyo alone is enormous. Here it is difficult to know what degree of merit to assign, as the sheer footage of abstract canvas turned out by Japanese 'modern' artists per year must exceed that of any other country, including France, and the difficulty is to detect an originality that may be described as truly Japanese. The care given to the display of paintings and sculpture is exemplary: every big department store in the country, but particularly those of Tokyo and Osaka, has its art gallery, where attention to lighting and temperature is scrupulous. And displays are held all the year round. Needless to say, the public galleries themselves are outstanding in their construction and in the quality of their exhibits; and when there is a major display, particularly of foreign works of art, the queues outside can stretch for as much as a mile. Meanwhile, art books, exquisitely produced, have a ready sale. As to architecture, Tange Kenzō and Maekawa Kunio are men of world standing.

Perhaps the public for Western music is greater even than it is for Western art. There are supposed to be more records of Western classical music sold in Japan than in any other country. This is remarkable when it is borne in mind that classical Japanese music is so thoroughly different in style from that of Europe. Nor is this addiction merely a pose or the result of a craze for anything Western, as some of the devotion to the extremes of abstract art may possibly be: anyone who has observed young people in cafés listening to Beethoven or Mozart must come to the conclusion that a genuine aesthetic need is being satisfied. There are many composers in the Western manner, but again it is difficult to say whether yet a Japanese style has emerged. What one can say is that Japanese executants are showing, in their tours abroad, a command of the medium which is truly remarkable.

One last word on the subject of religion. In an opinion poll conducted in 1957, 88 per cent of Japanese said that they had no religious beliefs; that is to say, this number replied No to the question 'Have you a religion?' The high proportion of negatives is startling; but there is some reason for caution in interpreting opinion polls, especially on matters of 'ultimate concern', and especially in Japan, where there is a reluctance to disclose innermost thoughts. It is interesting to compare the results of a similar enquiry undertaken in France in 1970. Although the French, and especially Frenchmen, are supposed to be much affected by scepticism, 85 per cent of French men and women more than twenty years old replied that they were Catholic, despite the fact that Mass is attended by only 21 per cent of the population. The high proportion is as surprising as the low proportion in the case of Japan, especially as there is an important Protestant minority in France; but two points need to be stressed, namely, the greater readiness of the French to declare themselves, and the use of the word Catholic to convey a general attitude rather than an explicit set of beliefs. If the Japanese had been asked, not 'Have you a religion?' but 'Are you religious?' it is possible, though for the reason given it is by no means certain, that the proportion of affirmative answers would have been far higher. It is by no means certain, because the individual Japanese is not accustomed to explicit formulation of what he thinks.[19]

If the reverence for beauty, and indeed for life in all its forms, is taken to be part of religion, as must be the sense of the sacred, then the Japanese are undoubtedly religious. Indeed, their whole *attitude* might be considered to be rather more religious, in the fundamental sense, than many a people professing a particular creed. Admittedly, visitors to Japan, at least those who stay long enough to be entitled to express an opinion, disagree among themselves as to whether religion means anything to the Japanese; but one is inclined to take the view just expressed, that in so far as religion carries the old meaning of *natural* religion, they are profoundly religious. They may not believe in religion as revelation, but that is because the whole world is a revelation to them. For this, they feel a kind of gratitude rarely evinced by others, who tend to take the world for granted. The childlike side of the Japanese character, which has often been remarked upon, means that they continue to take a wide-eyed view of life. Hence the importance of ceremony and ritual, even the little ceremonies and rituals of present-giving in everyday life, which, though sometimes tending towards artificiality and convention, imply ultimately a sacramental view of existence. In so far as it would not occur to a Japanese to view the world otherwise, it would not necessarily occur to him to define his attitude. It would be as if he were to attribute the mechanism of staying alive to eating and drinking, while forgetting about breathing.

One of the most powerful arguments for assigning an important part to religion in Japanese life, however, is the fact that, despite the apparent swing away from traditional beliefs since the war, a host of new religions have sprung up, known as *Shinkō-shūkyō*. These range from dignified and well-organized 'churches' to the most extraordinary efforts at revivalism, kept going by a man or woman convinced of having received divine favour, or even sometimes of divine incarnation. More than sixty such religions have been formally registered, and new ones are constantly being proclaimed. The growth and decline of many of these religions resemble those of political parties in some country struggling towards a democratic system; and naturally the validity of statistics in this sphere is sometimes open to challenge – no one likes to admit that the faithful are diminishing. Some religions were perhaps better described as forms of humanism; they concentrate above all on health and happiness in this world. Others, such as Seichō-no-Ie Kyōdan, are combinations of Shintō, Buddhism and Christianity. Many are liberally endowed with funds by enthusiastic adherents, and their headquarters are impressive, if often somewhat outlandish, edifices. This applies above all to Sōka-Gakkai or Value-Adding Society, with its political arm of Kōmeito or Clean Government party, founded in 1967: the religion based upon the teaching of Nichiren (p. 24), which some observers regard with considerable apprehension. Whatever its Buddhist theology, Sōka-Gakkai dwells much upon happiness and prosperity in this world; and it has made great headway in the Diet. Opposed to this belligerent religion is PL Kyōdan, or the Church of Permanent Liberty. Its founder, Miki Tokuchika, expresses his point of view in such utterances as 'Life is Art' or 'Life is a series of self-expressions', somewhat suggestive of Walter Pater. Indeed, many of the new religions appeal to the masses, and especially to the new middle-classes, in a manner which holds out hope of self-liberation and personal success; but apart from attending services and engaging in social work, there is little personal effort required of the devotee.

In dwelling upon *Shinkō-shūkyō*, we must not forget older 'new' religions. Of these one of the most remarkable is Tenri-kyō, founded by a not particularly well-to-do housewife, Mrs Nakayama Miki (1798-1887). Tenri-kyō is unique in that its founder claimed to be the incarnation of God, the first woman to do so. Mrs Nakayama's followers were persecuted in her time; but so magnetic was her personality that the cult grew, and it now has several million adherents, including many in Korea and South America. Its head-quarters are near Nara, and they include a large university, with an astonishingly rich library. To the faithful, Mrs Nakayama is not dead, but still 'in the world': therefore her invisible presence is ritually fed and put to bed every evening.

Almost all such religions lay particular stress on personal rectitude, and the means to attaining it – meditation, lustration etc. There is an argument, apparently endless, as to whether this emphasis on virtue implies a sense of sin. The Japanese are credited with a sense of shame, but not of sin or guilt, at least in the Christian sense. It is true that the character for 'sin' in traditional Japanese resembles that for 'crime'; but this does not necessarily mean that the notion of guilt is absent from the Japanese mentality. When anthropologists make statements about the absence of this or that quality from a people's 'soul', they are usually referring to differences of emphasis. Shame undoubtedly plays a very important part in Japanese culture; hence the importance given to 'face-saving'. But face-saving is emphasized in Western culture too, often more than is supposed. Studies made recently of the Japanese attitude to religion suggest that the attitude of contrition and unworthiness is just as strong in the East as in the West, and perhaps stronger.[20]

Whatever may be the truth concerning sin and shame, in relation to the Japanese religious mentality, the Japanese have practised for many centuries forms of religious meditation which, from the Western point of view, belong to mysticism. The Japanese mind is intuitive, but it is also introspective; and the aim of introspection is to seek inner harmony with the cosmic law. Once this is obtained, guilt and shame will have been overcome. At the same time, there is in the Japanese character a marked tendency to social idealism. This is brought out in the new religions, but it seems to develop at an early age, as Japanese children's essays and students' speeches make clear. Possibly this impulse towards idealism is the natural reaction to years in which Japan was thrown in upon herself; it is certainly more marked among the girls than among the boys, perhaps because the female mind finds little nourishment in radical, and especially Marxist, doctrine. If Japan is destined to be a leader in Asia, this impulse towards social betterment may be put to fruitful use; for if any part of the world exists where alleviating work needs to be done, it is there.

Notes on the text

1   PREHISTORY AND MYTH

1   Maurice Bairy, 'Japanese Ways', in *Doing Business in Japan*, p. 12.
2   *Things Japanese* (1905), pp. 7, 8.
3   It is now generally agreed that ancestor-worship was not originally part of the Shintō cult, but an importation from China. A recent statement from the Imperial Household Agency repudiated the suggestion that the Emperor enjoyed any official status in the Shintō religion; but the above observation still holds.
4   E.g. Geoffrey Bownas, *Japanese Rainmaking and other Folk Practices* (1963), p. 22.
5   It must be borne in mind that this was made possible by the absence of a strict law of succession, the frequency of abdication, and the fact that Emperors were polygamous and had numerous children.
6   This date is being pushed back as new archaeological evidence comes to light.
7   *Ebisu, emishi* and also *ezo* are supposed to be Ainu words for 'man'. Hokkaido was called *Ezo* or *Yezo* until the late nineteenth century. Before making mention of the Japanese, the Chinese called the Ainu *Mao Min*, 'hairy men'.
8   It has been pointed out that the 'crossing place' may well refer to the sea between Shimonoseki and Moji in the north of Kyushu, where the currents are exceptionally strong.
9   See Munro, *Ainu Creed and Cult* (1962), Appendix 1, p. 161.

2   THE NARA AND HEIAN PERIODS

1   An enthralling picture of that life is given in Ivan Morris's *World of the Shining Prince* (1964).

2 Ivan Morris renders *mono no aware* as *lacrimae rerum (op. cit.,* Appendix 6).
3 *The Lotus and the Robot* (London, 1960), p. 271.

1 'Go' in this context means 'the second'.

1 The military class in fact included the *daimyo.* In due course, the word 'samurai' covered the whole class.
2 It is estimated that there are over two million Japanese in the *Burakumin,* or 'special communities'.
3 The Chronicles date this as 604, but it may well have been written after the Prince's death, as a memorial to him (see Sir George Sansom, *A History of Japan,* Vol. 1 (1963), p. 51).
4 A novel such as Tanizaki Junichiro's *Some Prefer Nettles* (1928) reveals the extent to which Osaka had become the bourgeoisie's 'cultural centre'.
5 Translated by R. H. Blyth.
6 Yes, there are. Prince Hitachi, the Emperor's second son, wrote one about a tanker:

> The Shinano flows
> Through the mist of rain
> And an oil tanker
> Is ready to leave

and there are no doubt others.
7 There is a god of the water-closet or *benjo*, Ususama.
8 When they became acquainted with it, the Japanese despised Western writing. Tōin Shionoya (1810-67) described it as 'confused and irregular, wriggling like snakes or larvae of mosquitoes'.
9 Sir George Sansom, *A Short Cultural History of Japan* (1952), p. 483.
10 Quoted in Sansom, *A History of Japan,* Vol. III (1969), p. 99.
11 Quoted in Herryman Mauver, *Collision of East and West* (1951), p. 87.
12 Ronald Dore, *Education in Tokugawa Japan* (1965), p. 19.
13 Perhaps the best account in English of the forty-seven *rōnin* is that by A. B. Mitford, Lord Redesdale, in his *Tales of Old Japan,* and available in *Oriental Tales of Terror,* edited by J. J. Strating (London, 1971).

1   Quoted as an appendix to Lafcadio Hearn's *Japan: An Interpretation* (1905).

7   FROM MEDIEVAL TO MODERN

1   *Things Japanese* (1891), p. 1.
2   Nevertheless, loyal *daimyo* got extra stipends. In 1876, however, all samurai had to commute their rice stipends for cash or bonds.
3   Nakane Chie, *Kinship and Economic Organization in Rural Japan* (1967), p. 2.
4   *Ibid.*, p. 5.
5   The name Hokkaido was adopted in 1869.
6   Sir George Sansom, *Japan and the Western World* (1932), p. 398.
7   Marius B. Jansen, *Changing Japanese Attitudes towards Modernization* (1969), p. 66.
8   They were called Boxers because they cultivated special posture-boxing, which was supposed to render them invincible.
9   The expression was used originally during the Ashikaga Shogunate, i.e. the Kemmu Restoration (1334-36): see p. 36.

8   CO-PROSPERITY AND WAR

1   *The True Face of Japan*, p. 278.
2   Joseph C. Grew, *Ten Years in Japan* (1944), p. 177.
3   *Ibid.*, pp. 136, 165, 292 and 318.
4   John Toland, *The Rising Sun: the Rise and Fall of the Japanese Empire* (1970), p. 132.
5   *Ibid.*, p. 167.
6   *Ibid.*, p. 163.
7   Joseph C. Grew, *op. cit.*, p. 383.
8   Both Bergamini and Toland believe that not only General Homma but General Matsui and General Yamashita were unjustly sentenced after the war.
9   *Cf.* Herbert Feis, *The Atomic Bomb and the End of World War II* (1966), p. 7.
10 *Cf.* Robert J. Lifton, *Death in Life, the Survivors of Hiroshima* (1967), p. 38.

1   In fact, the ancient Emperors never claimed to be divine. Their descent from the sun-goddess was promulgated by nationalists from about the fourteenth century onwards.

2   After the war, each prefecture was required to have its own university. Many institutions were upgraded in status. The number of universities in the country therefore ran into hundreds.

3   *Cf.* P. B. Stone, *Japan Surges Ahead, Japan's Economic Rebirth* (1969), p. 12.

10   THE ECONOMIC MIRACLE

1   P. B. Stone, *op. cit.*, p. 55.

2   This is constantly repeated. See, for example, 'The Rush Hour of the Gods', by Charles Allen, in *The Listener*, 10 June 1971.

3   *E.g.* 'Let's put all our strength and mind together
    Doing our best to promote production'
                    (the Matsushita morning hymn).

4   Although this is well below European standards, the progressive rise is striking. The individual income level in Japan in 1955 was 11 per cent that of the United States, 27 per cent that of the UK, and 38 per cent that of Western Germany. But in 1969 it had risen to 34 per cent, 86 per cent, and 63 per cent respectively.

5   As English is Japan's language for all its transactions with the outside world, these ministries and other bodies are known by English titles.

6   *Consider Japan*, by correspondents of *The Economist* (1963), p. 48.

7   *Bulletin of the Anglo-Japanese Economic Institute*, No. 126, March 1972, p. 3.

8   As many as 16,278 people were killed in road accidents in 1971.

9   Toyota has a fleet of sea-going car-carriers, which can handle 160,000 exports cars per year. They sail from a special Toyota pier at Nagoya.

10   See 'A Challenge from Hiroshima' (*Sunday Times*, 4 February 1968).

11   Kitamura Hiroshi, 'Japan's Economic Policy towards South-East Asia' (*Proceedings of the Central Asian Society*, February 1972, p. 48).

11   JAPANESE LIFE AND THOUGHT

1   A kind of loose kimono, padded in winter.

2   Among the most powerful women today are Mrs Murayama, who

controls the *Asahi Shimbun*, and her daughter, Miss Murayama Michi, who organizes the annual Osaka International Festival.

3 Sugimoto Etsu Inagaki, *A Daughter of the Samurai* (1926), p. 178.

4 In 1893, a foreign observer, Henry Norman (*The Real Japan*, p. 177) could write: 'The very vocabulary of romantic love does not exist in Japanese.' This is certainly not true today.

5 Yoshida Kenkō (1283-1350), 'Essays in Idleness' (*Anthology of Japanese Literature*, edited by Donald Keene, pp. 220-221).

6 *The Japanese are Like That* (1965), p. 134.

7 Translated by Sydney Giffard, 1955.

8 Bowing is an extremely old custom in Japan, and it is mentioned in the early Chinese chronicles. *Cf.* Sir George Sansom, *Japan, a Short Cultural History* (1962), pp. 30-31.

9 According to the *Bulletin of the Anglo-Japanese Economic Institute* (No. 21, October 1971), a Tokyo business school discovered that most of the girl students wished to take jobs giving them the opportunity of work abroad.

10 Figures for 1971. Less than 20 per cent of houses have toilets with running water.

11 *The Japanese Challenge* (1970), pp. 115-17.

12 It was in fact challenged vigorously by an American critic, Roy Andrew Miller in the *Virginia Quarterly Review*, Spring 1971, p. 288.

13 'The Japanese architect... except of course for the designer of the twentieth-century department store and office block, has never quite come to terms with the chill of the snow and the winter winds of his new northern home' (Geoffrey Bownas, *Japanese Rainmaking and other Folk Practices* (1963), p. 14.

14 *Cf.* Lewis Bush, *Japanalia* (1960), p. 85.

15 Traditionally, houses contained a small Shintō and Buddhist shrine on shelves one above the other. They are still to be seen, especially in the country.

16 In the Philippines, the International Research Institute, aided by the Rockefeller and Ford Foundations, has developed a 'miracle rice' of nearly equal yield. See Raymond Nelson, *The Philippines* in this series (1968), p. 145.

17 The drink most popular at the moment is beer. In 1971, the average annual per capita consumption was 67.8 bottles of beer, 12.2 bottles of *sake* and 2.7 bottles of whisky.

18 *The Times*, 16 March 1971.

19 Observers often contradict themselves on this issue. *Cf.* two statements at the beginning and at the end of *Changing Japan*, by Edward Norbeck (1965):

'It is a nation where life is secular, where most of the citizenry disclaims faith in any religion' (p. 1).

'Many people regard themselves as being religious' (p. 47).

20 See *Japanese Youth Confronts Religion*, Fernando M. Basabe (1967), and 'Technique and Personal Devotion in the Zen Exercises', by Heinrich Dumoulin in *Studies in Japanese Culture*, edited by Joseph Roggendorf (1963).

Glossary

AIKIDŌ one of the traditional martial arts

BAKUFU lit., 'tent government': the Shogun's government

BUNRAKU puppet drama

BURAKUMIN outcaste villages

BUSHI military caste

BUSHIDŌ military code: code of the warrior

CHA'AN Chinese word from which Zen was derived

CHA-NO-YU Tea Ceremony

CHIU-KUSHII Ainu for 'rapid stream or crossing place': possible origin of the old word for Kyushu (*Tsukushi*)

CHŪ loyalty to the Emperor

DAIMYO feudal lord

ETA outcastes

GEKOKUJŌ 'rule of the higher by the lower', used especially of officers in the 1930's who presented their superiors with *faits accomplis*

GENIN members of family household not related by blood

GENRŌ 'elder statesmen' who chose the prime minister during the Meiji era

GIRI duty, obligation

GONIN-GUMI 'five-man group' of samurai

HAIKU poem of seventeen syllables (5:7:5), usually about the passing of the seasons

HAN domain

HANIWA cylinders of pottery on which stand figures of men, beasts or dwellings, often found in ancient tombs

HIBAKUSHA name for the survivors of the atom bomb attacks on Hiroshima and Nagasaki

HIRAGANA one of the two syllabaries of the Japanese language

IE collective household

IKEBANA flower-arrangement

INKYŌ system whereby the parents left the family house to the young married couple and settled in a smaller house on the same property

JŪNIN-GUMI 'ten-man group' of peasants

KAKEMONO inscribed scroll usually hung in the *tokonoma*

KAMA curved dagger, often used by samurai women

KAMI lit., 'superior ónes': Shintō gods

KAMIKAZE lit., 'divine wind': used first of the tempest that destroyed the Mongol fleet

KAMUI Ainu word for 'gods'

KAMUI-FUCHI the Ainu 'Great Ancestress'

KEN prefecture

KENDŌ one of the traditional martial arts

KIRISUTE lit., 'to cut down and leave' (samurai habit in dealing with enemies or with those obstructing their path)

KŌ artisans

KŌAN Zen riddle or conundrum

KOKUGAKU national learning

KŌNOMONO mixed pickles or preserved vegetables

O-MATSURI festival

MONO-NO-AWARE 'lacrimae rerum' (Ivan Morris's rendering)

NAGINATA long spear with curved blade, often used by samurai women

NAKŌDO match-maker or go-between

NEMBUTSU invocation of the Buddha

NĒSAN lit., elder sister: waitress in café

NŌ peasants

NORI seaweed beaten into thin leaves, 'like carbon paper' (Moch Joya)

OBI sash for binding kimono

OKASHI a 'pretty wit', as displayed by Sei Shōnagon

OKU-SAN 'mistress of the household': wife

ON indebtedness, usually to one's superior, for favours received

ONSEN hot-spring or spa

OYABUN-KOBUN system of personal relationships with a distinct paternalistic character and corresponding loyalty of subordinates

RANGAKU Dutch learning

RŌNIN lit., 'masterless men', who wandered the country when the samurai system was breaking up

RYOKAN Japanese inn

SAKE rice wine: the 'sacred' drink of Japan

SANKIN-KŌTAI 'alternate attendance': practice adopted by the Tokugawa Shoguns to ensure loyalty of *daimyo*

SASHIMI raw fish

SATORI Zen enlightenment, following upon meditation or the propounding of a *kōan*

O-SEMBEI salted biscuit or cracker, often surrounded by a band of seaweed

SEPPUKU hara-kiri, ritual suicide by disembowelment

SHI military caste

SHINKŌ-SHŪKYŌ new religions

SHINTŌ the primordial faith of Japan

SHIRATAKI food resembling macaroni or noodles

SHŌ merchants

SOBA buckwheat noodles

SŌNNŌ JŌI 'Revere the Emperor, expel the barbarians': an anti-Tokugawa slogan before the Meiji Restoration

SUKIYAKI beef, pork or chicken in thin slices cooked in soy sauce with vegetables, *shirataki*, bean-curd and sugar

SUSHI 'little patties of rice savoured with vinegar surmounted by strips (or slabs in expensive *sushiya*) of raw fish, octopus, squid, a kind of omelet, and a variety of other tidbits' (*Japanese Cooking*, by Peter and Joan Martin, 1970, p. 56)

TATAMI straw matting about six feet long and three feet wide, bound with cloth, and used for floor covering

TEMPURA fish etc. dipped in batter and fried in sesame oil

T'IEN Chinese : 'heaven'

TŌFU bean curd

TOKONOMA alcove or recess in which a picture or scroll (*kakemono*) is hung or flower-arrangement placed. The guest always sits with his back to the *tokonoma*

UJI clan

UKIYO the 'floating world' (of actors, courtesans, etc.)

UKIYO-E woodblock prints largely depicting the above

WAGŌ social harmony

WAKŌ pirates

YUKATA house-kimono padded in winter, or used for walking outdoors in summer

ZA merchant guild

ZAIBATSU big business houses or cartels: the current Japanese word is *zaikai*

ZAZEN Zen meditation and the sitting posture associated with it

Who's Who

ADAMS, William (1564–1620). Shipwrecked on the coast of Kyushu in 1600, being navigator on a Dutch vessel. Tokugawa Ieyasu befriended him, and he not only built ships for his master but also became his confidential adviser on trade and on relations in general with foreign countries. He was granted an estate and married a Japanese, though he had a wife at home. His plea to return to England after five years' stay in Japan was refused. He died while visiting the English factory at Hirado, north-west of Nagasaki, and he and his wife were buried at Tsukayama, Miura region, where an annual commemorative ceremony on April 14th is still held.

BASHŌ Matsuo (1644–94). Of minor samurai descent, in 1653 Bashō became a page in the Tōdō family, where a warm friendship sprang up between himself and Yoshitada, the heir of the family. Yoshitada died in 1666, and Bashō, much grieved by his death, left for Kyoto, where he is said to have lived in the Kinpukuji Temple, studying the Japanese classics and calligraphy, but also writing *haiku* of a new and original kind. In 1671, he produced an anthology of verse, with his own critical comments; and the following year he left for Edo, where he seems to have undergone a profound spiritual experience, which led him to the practice of Zen meditation. He is regarded as one of Japan's greatest poets.

CHIKAMATSU Monzaemon (1653–1724). Playwright, generally regarded as the Shakespeare of Japan. His early dramas are popular versions of Noh plays, but in due course he changed from artificial language to a more realistic form, and excelled in the depiction of character and the analysis of psychological states.

FUKUZAWA Yūkichi (1834–1901). Devoted his life to the study of Western culture and science, wrote a number of books on educational ideas, and founded Keio University in Tokyo. His autobiography is a fascinating book, essential reading for anyone who would understand the emergence of the New Japan. (See *The Japanese Enlightenment : a Study of the Writings of Fukuzawa Yūkichi*, by Carmen Blacker.)

HEARN, Lafcadio (1850–1904). Commissioned to write a series of articles on Japan, he arrived in that country in 1890; but he abandoned his contract and began to teach at the Matsue Middle School. During his time in Matsue, perhaps the happiest in his life, he married a Japanese lady. He then moved to Kumamoto, where he taught in the High School, and later worked on a newspaper in Kobe. Finally, he became a lecturer in English at the Tokyo Imperial University. Hearn's writings were the first, and possibly the most successful, to interpret Japan to the Western world. Many scholars now regard his 'interpretation' as romantic and sentimental, but few would deny his remarkable insight and the elegance of his literary style.

HIDEYOSHI Toyotomi (1537–98). Son of a poor farmer, as a youth he was restless and difficult to discipline, and he tried various occupations without success until he was appointed sandal-keeper and later assistant to Nobunaga Oda. He proved a brave soldier and defeated a number of Nobunaga's enemies. On learning of the latter's death, he turned upon the assassins and soon became as powerful as his former master. In 1596 he was appointed Prime Minister, but shortly afterwards resigned the office to his adopted son, and prepared to wage a campaign of conquest against Korea and China. Before his generals had completed their task, Hideyoshi died. He was a great builder of castles, two of the most important being Osaka and Fushimi. Like Nobunaga, he was devoted to the Tea Ceremony, and he had a genuine appreciation of the arts. He was hostile to Christianity.

HIROSHIGE (1787–1855). Son of an employee of the Shogun, he showed a precocious aptitude for art, and became a pupil of Utagawa Toyohiro, famous *ukiyo-e* painter, though he had hoped to study under Hokusai himself. He rose to fame with his *Tōkaidō Gojūsan-Tsugi* or 'Fifty-three stations of the Tōkaidō', and thereafter he produced a succession of woodblock prints of remarkable beauty.

HOKUSAI Katsushika (1760–1849). Early apprenticed to a wood engraver, he later studied under the painter Shunshō but his originality was such that he incurred the jealousy of his master and was dismissed. There followed a period of great difficulty, when he hawked calendars in the street; but a timely legacy enabled him to continue as an artist, and he began to attract considerable attention. In 1817, he published the first of the *Hokusai Manga* ('Hokusai Cartoons'), a remarkable series of prints of familiar scenes, birds, animals, flowers, etc. Late in life he produced the series for which he is best known, the 'Thirty-seven views of Mount Fuji'.

ITŌ Hirobumi (1841–1909). Japan's first Prime Minister (1885–88) after the Meiji Restoration, he was one of the framers of the Meiji Constitution, and he based many of his recommendations on his knowledge of Germany. (He was an admirer of Bismarck.) In 1900, he founded the Minsei Kai, one of the important political parties prior to the Second World War. He was a firm upholder of the policy of attaching Korea to Japan, and was Resident-General there, as Prince Itō, 1905–09. Assassinated by a Korean nationalist.

KITTA Ikki (1884–1937). Prominent right-wing revolutionary, who advocated a social philosophy very like National Socialism. He also sought to propagate the idea of a revolution in Asia under Japanese leadership. In 1919, he wrote *An Outline Plan for the Reconstruction of Japan*. This, like his other inflammatory writings, was officially suppressed, but they were nevertheless read widely, especially among the young officers. He never attacked the Emperor system. After an incident involving officers of the *Kōdō* or Imperial Way group in February 1936, in which he was thought to have played a part, he was executed.

MISHIMA Yukio (1925–70). Educated at the Peers' School, Tokyo, where he came under the influence of the Japanese romanticists, Mishima never ceased to revere the virtues of the old martial spirit of Japan. His first book, a collection of short stories published during the war, when he was nineteen, revealed with extreme frankness his homosexual tendencies. Under the influence of European literature, and especially Mauriac, he began to write less 'personal' novels, and also a stream of short stories and some plays (from 1948 onwards), including experiments in modern Noh drama. The novel *The Temple of the Golden Pavilion* proved a great success both in and outside Japan, and soon Mishima was recognized as Japan's leading novelist, whom many thought deserving of the Nobel Prize. *After the Banquet* and the moving short story *Patriotism* show Mishima's preoccupation with tradition again, and a little later he established a patriotic group called the Shield Society, to 'shield' the Emperor. His crowning work was a novel dealing with the theme of reincarnation, called *The Sea of Fertility*. He seemed to feel that in this work he had said all he had to say, and he hinted that his next act would be his own death. This he brought about after vainly haranguing the armed forces on the evils of materialism and Westernization. He committed hara-kiri in the orthodox samurai manner.

MURASAKI Shikibu (c.975–c.1025). Lady Murasaki was a member of the Fujiwara family, and became a lady-in-waiting at Court. Well versed in the Chinese and Buddhist classics, she kept a diary for a brief period (1008–10), and this shows that at the end of her life she cherished a simple faith in Amida Buddha. She married probably in 999, but her husband died in 1001. Her remarkable novel *The Tale of Genji* (begun probably about 1002 and continued until 1020) portrays life at the Fujiwara-dominated Court; and although it is mostly concerned with amorous intrigues, it displays a refinement of sensibility and a delicate wit for which there are few, if any, parallels. It has been called 'the first psychological novel in the literature of the world'.

NAKAYAMA Miki (1798–1887). Founder of the Tenri-kyō ('Rule of Heaven') cult. In 1837, it was revealed to her in a trance that she was the 'True and Original God... descended from heaven to save all human beings'. She had several other revelations, in one of which she was enjoined to practise total poverty. She distributed almost all her worldly goods, and devoted herself to charitable work as well as to forms of 'spiritual healing'. Disciples multiplied, and she wrote voluminous scriptures, devised religious dances, and founded churches. Her death took place in 1887, but the faithful believe that she is still 'in the world'. The number of Tenri-kyō adherents, both in Japan and throughout the world, now totals several millions, and there are at least 15,000 churches. The headquarters of the sect is near Nara, where there is also a university with a museum and a particularly well-stocked library.

NICHIREN (1222–82). A militant Buddhist leader, born in a poor family of fisher-folk. He placed emphasis upon the *Lotus Sutra*, which he regarded as the essence of Buddhist teaching. He attacked other sects, especially that of Pure Land Buddhism, and declared that Buddhist heresies would be punished by foreign invasion. The arrival of the Mongols seemed to bear out his prediction, and his sect gained considerable support. His ideas acquired a nationalistic tinge, and the modern version of Nichiren Buddhism, Sōka-Gakkai, reveals a similar tendency.

NOBUNAGA Oda (1534–82). A feudal lord, descended from the Taira clan, who acquired power and influence by overcoming neighbouring *daimyo* and forming astute marriage alliances. In 1568, he entered Kyoto, overthrowing the Shogun, and spent the next decade in bringing the entire country under his own control. He had nearly succeeded in this aim when he was assassinated by one of his own generals. Throughout his life Nobunaga was loyal to the Emperor, who awarded him many honours. He built great castles, and restored the Imperial palace. Despite his immense power, he never formally assumed the title of Shogun. Nobunaga was in general favourable to the Christians, though he was not always tolerant of Buddhists, especially those who interfered in politics.

SAIGŌ Takamori (1827–77). One of the leaders of the group which overthrew the power of the Tokugawa Shogunate and brought about the Meiji Restoration of 1868. Later he found himself in violent conflict with ministers on the question of policy towards Korea, and as a result he resigned his office and returned to Kagoshima in Kyushu. Here he busied himself with establishing schools to provide a training for impoverished samurai. So great was his local power and prestige that the government of Tokyo felt obliged to assert its authority. Believing that Tokyo was conspiring against his life, Saigō resolved to overthrow the government, which at once declared him a rebel. Saigō's defiance was the last serious attempt by the samurai to retain their feudal privileges. He met with unexpectedly strong resistance, and realizing that his cause was lost, he committed hara-kiri.

SEI SHŌNAGON (966 or 967–1009?). Author of the famous *Makura-no-sōshi* or *Pillow Book*. Like Lady Murasaki, a Court lady. The diary which she kept covers the years 991–1000, not in a strict chronological sequence. She provides notes under such headings as 'disagreeable things', 'amusing things', 'things that make one happy' etc., and in recording them she displays considerable wit and much acute observation, giving a vivid picture of the life of her times, at least at the aristocratic level. Like Lady Murasaki, she wrote not in Chinese but in Japanese and in the *kana* syllabary. The two writers seem to have known each other, and in her diary Lady Murasaki makes some caustic remarks about Sei Shōnagon. Both the *Tale of Genji* and the *Pillow Book* have been translated, freely and only in part, by Arthur Waley; Ivan Morris has now issued a complete translation of the *Pillow Book*.

SESSHŪ (1420–1506). Attached to a temple at the age of 13. Sesshū revealed a marked talent for painting. He was accordingly sent to Kamakura for formal instruction. In 1467, he was sent to China and having been greatly influenced by Chinese art, he became the leading painter in the so-called *Nangwa*, or Chinese school. He perfected the black-and-white landscape style, and was the greatest of the artists working under the influence of Zen.

TANAKA Kakuei (b. 1918). Conscripted in 1939 and served in Manchuria. Returned to Japan in 1941 and was invalided out after pneumonia. After his recovery he set up a construction company and in the years 1942–49 he was commuting from Japan to Korea on business. Appointed Prime Minister after the resignation of Eisaku Sato in July 1972, he published *A Proposal for Remodelling the Japanese Archipelago*, which enjoyed an enormous sale. The book's appeal, and something of Tanaka's political idealism, can be judged from the following quotation: 'When more than 100 million competent, bright and diligent Japanese put all their strength together to solve inflation, pollution, overpopulation (in cities), underpopulation (in rural areas), stagnant agriculture and the generation gap common to developed countries, while avoiding militarism, the people of the world will find Japan in the van of civilization.' In September 1972, Tanaka met President Nixon in Honolulu, an encounter which revealed Japan for the first time since the war as having 'come of age' internationally. He also visited China, as a result of which relations between the two countries were normalized.

TŌGŌ Heihachiro (1847–1934). Generally regarded as Japan's foremost sailor. Received his naval education in England, being attached to the Thames Nautical College, H.M.S. *Worcester*, and making the voyage to Australia in an English sailing ship. He served with great distinction during the Sino-Japanese war of 1894. In 1905, during the Russo-Japanese war, he inflicted a crushing defeat on the Russians at the Battle of Tsushima, perhaps the most famous naval battle in Japanese history.

TŌJŌ Hideki (1884–1948). Graduating from the Military Staff College in 1915, Tōjō received rapid promotion, and in 1937 he became chief of staff of the Kwangtung Army, the force which, almost a law unto itself, conquered and exploited Manchukuo. In the second and third cabinets of Prince Konoe (1940 and

1941), he served as War Minister, and just before the outbreak of the Pacific War he became Prime Minister, while retaining his post at the War Ministry. After the fall of Saipan in the Marianas in 1944, he resigned. During his term of office he had exercised the functions of dictator of Japan. After being accused of war crimes, he was hanged in 1948.

TOKUGAWA Ieyasu (1542–1616). A vassal of both Nobunaga and Hideyoshi. When the latter died, his adopted son Hideyori succeeded him; but Ieyasu defeated him at the battle of Sekigahara in 1600 and established his headquarters in Edo (later Tokyo). Although the Emperor designated him Shogun, he held the title for only a few years before handing it over to his son Hidetada in 1605. Clearly, he wanted the title to remain in the Tokugawa family, and in fact it did so until 1868. At the age of 74, Ieyasu died, knowing that his family fortunes were secure. He was hostile to the Christians, like Hideyoshi, but his anti-Christian regulations were not at first strictly enforced. He was the patron of the Englishman Will Adams.

UMAYADO, Prince (574–622), posthumously named Shōtoku Taishi. Nephew of the Empress Suiko (who came to the throne in 592), he served as Regent for his aunt. A fervent Buddhist, he was a man of great learning and administrative ability, and during his term of office Buddhism became an established faith. In 604, he issued the proclamation known as the 'Seventeen Article Constitution', a blend of Buddhist and Confucian precepts, addressed chiefly to the ruling class, and embodying ideas of centralized government borrowed from China. In the same year he adopted the Chinese calendar, confirming 660 BC as the date of the foundation of the Japanese state, and later he sent political and cultural missions to China. Founded the Hōryūji temple near Nara.

YOSHIDA Shigeru (1878–1967). Japan's greatest post-war statesman. Presided over cabinets as Prime Minister in 1946, 1948, 1949, 1952, and 1953. During the Korean war, and at America's insistence, he cautiously permitted a degree of rearmament, though this violated Article 9 of the Constitution which the United States had imposed. At the end of his life, he had become a figure comparable to the *genrō* of the Meiji era. On his deathbed he was received into the Catholic Church.

Acknowledgments

The Historiographical Institute, University of Tokyo, 17; Imperial Household Collection, Kyoto, 7; Japan Information Centre, London, 1, 6, 8, 20, 21, 23, 25, 26, 28; Japan National Tourist Organization, 9, 18, 27; Fosco Maraini, 24; Ministry of Foreign Affairs, Tokyo, 22; Municipal Museum, Kobe, 12, 14; Collection, National Museum of Ethnology, Leiden, 3; Paul Popper, 19; Routledge & Kegan Paul Ltd, 11, 12; M. Suenaga, 5; Tokyo National Museum, 2, 4, 13; Victoria and Albert Museum, London, 15, 16; *Yomiuri Shimbun*, 29

Index